Crafting the Lyric Essay

Crafting the Lyric Essay

Strike a Chord

HEIDI CZERWIEC

BLOOMSBURY ACADEMIC
LONDON • NEW YORK • OXFORD • NEW DELHI • SYDNEY

BLOOMSBURY ACADEMIC
Bloomsbury Publishing Plc
50 Bedford Square, London, WC1B 3DP, UK
1385 Broadway, New York, NY 10018, USA
29 Earlsfort Terrace, Dublin 2, Ireland

BLOOMSBURY, BLOOMSBURY ACADEMIC and the Diana logo are trademarks of Bloomsbury Publishing Plc

First published in Great Britain 2024

Copyright © Heidi Czerwiec, 2024

Heidi Czerwiec has asserted her right under the Copyright, Designs and Patents Act, 1988, to be identified as Author of this work.

For legal purposes the Acknowledgments on p. ix constitute an extension of this copyright page.

Design and character illustration by Annabel Hewitson
Border image © Duncan1890/ iStock

All rights reserved. No part of this publication may be reproduced or transmitted in any form or by any means, electronic or mechanical, including photocopying, recording, or any information storage or retrieval system, without prior permission in writing from the publishers.

Bloomsbury Publishing Plc does not have any control over, or responsibility for, any third-party websites referred to or in this book. All internet addresses given in this book were correct at the time of going to press. The author and publisher regret any inconvenience caused if addresses have changed or sites have ceased to exist, but can accept no responsibility for any such changes.

A catalogue record for this book is available from the British Library.

Library of Congress Cataloging-in-Publication Data

Names: Czerwiec, Heidi (Heidi K.), author.
Title: Crafting the lyric essay : strike a chord / Heidi Czerwiec.
Description: London; New York: Bloomsbury Academic, 2024. | Includes bibliographical references and index.
Identifiers: LCCN 2023032731 (print) | LCCN 2023032732 (ebook) | ISBN 9781350383005 (paperback) | ISBN 9781350382992 (hardback) | ISBN 9781350383012 (pdf) | ISBN 9781350383029 (epub)
Subjects: LCSH: Essay–Authorship. | Creative nonfiction–Authorship.
Classification: LCC PN4500 .C94 2024 (print) | LCC PN4500 (ebook) | DDC 808.4–dc23/eng/20230814
LC record available at https://lccn.loc.gov/2023032731
LC ebook record available at https://lccn.loc.gov/2023032732

ISBN: HB: 978-1-3503-8299-2
PB: 978-1-3503-8300-5
ePDF: 978-1-3503-8301-2
eBook: 978-1-3503-8302-9

Typeset by Deanta Global Publishing Services, Chennai, India

To find out more about our authors and books visit www.bloomsbury.com and sign up for our newsletters.

*To Brenda, Nicole, and Lee for bushwhacking my path,
to Karen for helping me stack the cairns for the rest to follow,
and to everyone cited here—I'm so grateful for your words.*

CONTENTS

(traditional craft essay titles are in roman type; lyric craft essay titles are italicized)

Acknowledgments ix

Introduction 1

Consider the Lobster Mushroom 5

On Lateral Moves 9
Success in Circuit: Lyric Essay as Labyrinth 9
A Jump to the Left, and Then a Step to the Right: On Lateral Moves in the Lyric Essay 13

Lyric Time 21

On Uses of Space 31
Mind the Gap: Writing Around Absence 31
Negative Capability 37
Fragmentation Grenade: The Violence of Hybridity 55

A Dash of Dash: The Lyric Art of Punctuation 59

Permissive Sieves 63

On Resonance 67
Strike a Chord: The Lyre That Makes the Lyric 67
The Resonance of Lyric Essays, or Lyre, Not Liar 81

On the Image 85

Image Alt-Narratives: Deep-Diving, Mutating, and Chaining 85
Pushing Up Daisies: Three Image Alt-Narratives 95

On Poetic Forms 97

Using Poetic Forms in Creative Nonfiction 97
(R)Evolution Pantoum: Play with Your Food 101

The Four Temperaments of Creative Nonfiction 105

Revisiting Annie Dillard's *Holy the Firm* 115

Ekphragrance 119

On Structure 125

Structures of Thinking: Structure, Syntax, and Form in the Lyric Essay 125
Thinking Cap 140

Useful Distinctions, or, Why the Lyric Essay Is a Function, Not a Form 142

Epilogue: Recital 152

References 157
Suggested Reading List 165
Index 167

ACKNOWLEDGMENTS

This book wouldn't exist without Karen Babine and our Craft Cider colloquies, without the spurring on of Kate Nuernberger and parallel play with Jenn Gibbs, and without invaluable discussions with Randon Billings Noble, Joanna Eleftheriou, Nomi Stone, Beth Alvarado, and other partners in lyric essay crimes.

Much love goes out to Lucy Brown, Aanchal Vij, and the rest of the editorial team at Bloomsbury Publishing for their insight and help in guiding this manuscript from project to publication.

Big high-fives and gratitude to the following, where work from this book previously appeared:

Assay: The Journal of Nonfiction Studies, "Revisiting Annie Dillard's *Holy the Firm*," "Ekphragrance: On Using Smell in Writing and Teaching Nonfiction," "Using Poetic Forms in Nonfiction"

Bending Genre, "Permissive Sieves: Comparing the Ghazal and Lyric Essay as Forms"

Brevity's Nonfiction Blog: "Consider the Lobster Mushroom" and "(R)Evolution Pantoum: Play with Your Food"

CRAFT, "A Jump to the Left, Then a Step to the Right: Lateral Moves in the Lyric Essay"

Essay Daily's 2021 Advent Calendar: "The Resonance of Lyric Essays or Lyre, Not Liar"

Fourth Genre, "A Dash of Dash"

Hippocampus Magazine, "Of Fragments and Segments" (an excerpt of "Negative Capability")

River Teeth's "Beautiful Things": "Zero at the Bone" (an excerpt of "Mind the Gap")

Sweet: A Literary Confection, "Fragmentation Grenade: The Violence of Hybridity"

"Consider the Lobster Mushroom" first appeared in *Brevity*'s blog and was published in the essay collection *Fluid States*, Pleiades Press, 2019.

"Success in Circuit: Lyric Essay as Labyrinth" first appeared in *A Harp in the Stars: An Anthology of Lyric Essays*, ed. Randon Billings Noble, University of Nebraska Press, 2021.

Introduction

Karen and I sat on the back deck, piles of books at our feet, talking taxonomies, bemoaning the lack of a shared critical vocabulary in creative nonfiction, craft essays, and venues for publishing them, because not enough people were writing them and we need them. In fact, that's why Karen started the invaluable *Assay: A Journal of Nonfiction Studies*, to create such a venue and publish the work we need. We bounced ideas off each other for craft essays for the *Assay* blog, bounced bottlecaps off the slats as we opened bottles of cold cider. She was thinking through the energy of turns in writing, based on the metaphor of the fouetté, how the physics propels the piece in a new direction. I was thinking about labyrinths, and how the turns and movement might not be so apparent—how the lyric essay may move laterally, through juxtaposition and accretion, traveling great distances within a small space—which wasn't at all helpful for Karen's piece. She approached via narrative and linear essays, whereas I was talking lyric. Over more weekends and more ciders and more of me saying, "Well, that doesn't really apply to lyric writing," she'd reply, "then you should write about it." I said there's already lots of writing on the lyric, this isn't anything new. Karen said, it's new to us: "you need to explain how lyric craft is being used in creative nonfiction, because not enough people are doing it and we need it."

We both agreed to pursue our separate critical threads and to keep showing each other work, at least once a month. We called it Craft Cider.

I felt like I was cheating. I need to establish a couple of things. I came late to creative nonfiction, after decades of writing, training, teaching, and researching as a poet. I'm still playing catch-up with the standards of nonfiction craft, even as nonfiction craft is playing catch-up with the body of work in other genres. But Karen convinced me what I bring to the discourse is a deep familiarity with the craft techniques of poetry. I'd bring up a lyric strategy, and she'd say "Explain it to me like I'm ten," which utterly misrepresents how smart she is. But her point was that, despite an MFA and a critical background in creative nonfiction, she didn't know what I meant until I described how it worked. For instance, in talking about turns, I'd reference seminal poet-critic John Hollander's "Some Notes on Refrain" to explain how a piece might return to refrain as a sonic focal point before spinning off in a new direction. Karen was excited by my explanation, but said she wasn't familiar with Hollander and no one was making those connections, which seemed necessary for understanding the lyric essay. The lyric essay is achieving a critical mass in publication, yet the critical work explaining its workings lags. Because so many writers of the lyric essay also come to it from poetry, it makes sense to import discussions of poetic craft when it's useful to help explain various aspects of how the lyric essay functions on the page. I don't pretend these discussions are new, but thanks to Karen, *la migliore fabbra*, I'm persuaded they *are* new to creative nonfiction, and I'm hoping to provoke and facilitate what I see as a necessary and useful conversation.

Given the conversations I've been having, there is a clear hunger for thoughtful work on the topic. Too often, a fundamental misunderstanding of the term "lyric" leads to it being deployed to label any nonfiction using forms and techniques not common in prose, anything quirky and/or short, or even to excuse lazy writing. This collection aims to remedy that in specific terms, by arguing (like Judith Kitchen) that the lyric essay depends on the lyre, on lyric mode—a focus on patterning, and on resonances of sound and silence and image on the level of the language. As the lyric essay is becoming a hot subject, this book is an opportunity to move that conversation forward—a conversation largely dominated by John D'Agata who, upon attaching himself to Deborah Tall's coining of the term, via *The Next American Essay* and after, seems to want to trademark it, to make it his brand. That's not a conversation; it's a monologue. My craft book arose out of conversations, some portrayed in these pages, and I hope it will spark ongoing discussion.

Many of the essays themselves are in conversation with each other, presented in the form of paired essays, as indicated in the Table of Contents and in the titling of the pieces themselves: a hybrid craft essay embodies the lyric craft element being studied, while a more traditional craft essay reviews relevant lyric theory and craft and applies it to examples of the lyric essay. As such, this book invites you to read it in any number of ways: start to finish, jumping around, reading the lyric craft essays (titles italicized) for your own pleasure, consulting the craft essays with a group of advanced writers and/or students for a deeper dive into the applications of lyric theory and poetics, or considering one of the paired essay sets to study how one embodies and enacts the craft analyzed in the other. Some example texts are used for multiple craft topics, so you can highlight particular strategies but also see how individual strategies work together. A list of these readings is provided at the end and, happily, many are available online so you easily can access and study the full text alongside the discussions.

I'm excited by moves to theorize about the essay form. At a moment when nonfiction is proliferating and hybridizing in exciting ways, and craft techniques are being borrowed and adapted from other genres and mediums, craft is a huge and necessary part of the discussion. So, it makes me supremely happy to see nonfiction thinking about itself in such well-articulated ways. I hope this book adds to that conversation, and I hope we continue to see more.

Consider the Lobster Mushroom

Being a Brief Theory of the Craft of Creative Nonfiction

The lobster mushroom, contrary to its common name, is not a mushroom but the result of a parasitic fungus having infested a host mushroom in a peculiar symbiosis. The fungus, *Hypomyces lactifluorum*, typically attacks milk-caps and brittlegills, absorbing them completely and imparting the bright reddish-orange color and seafood-like flavor of a cooked lobster.

Creative nonfiction, too, is a symbiosis of fact infecting art. Or art infecting fact. You become infected by an idea, a topic—open adoptions, fracking, the history of perfume—that absorbs you, imparting its own qualities, until you're transformed, not the same person as before.

Or, you may play the part of parasite—cloak your work, make it take the appearance of another form: an essay disguised as a list, a letter, an index, a diary. A hermit crab essay. A lobster mushroom.

Or, you may think you're writing one essay, but another essay takes it over, makes it its own. Think you're writing about hiking? Nope, it's about your ex-. A piece about the band Morphine and *The Matrix*'s Morpheus and the *Sandman* comics? Nope, your ex-. This is not necessarily a bad thing. Lobster mushrooms are much more valuable than the mushrooms they infect—about $25 a pound fresh, or $50 dried, at last check.

* * *

You should remember both creative nonfiction and lobster mushrooms, like all fungus, feed off dead matter, are in turn fed off of. You don't always get there first. Sometimes appalling creatures have nested inside it—sometimes stuff you knew was there, sometimes stuff you forgot was there, sometimes unexpected stuff you uncover. You might be cutting through a mushroom when a centipede or earwig or worm crawls out of the hole it's burrowed into the flesh. "Fuck!" you might yell, dropping the mushroom. Now you have to decide what to do next:

- a) Sweep the mushroom into the trash. Burn trash. Burn house. No mushroom, no matter how valuable it might have seemed, is worth this toxic invasion.
- b) Pick up the mushroom and examine the damage—How deep does it go? Has the nastiness laid eggs? Are there others? You may feel hesitant to give up on the mushroom, but sometimes you have to negotiate the value of the mushroom against how compromised it's become. If there's too much damage, go back to a); otherwise, continue to c). Remind yourself of two things:
  1. If you can't deal with the mushroom now, it will come back. It will always come back, popping up whether you want it to or no, because it's part of a larger system, mycelia feeding on what's rotten, what lurks, always, beneath the surface. If you decide in the future you're ready to pluck it and make something of it, it will be there, mushrooming.
  2. You don't have to reveal the source of your mushrooms. Few enthusiasts do, going to great lengths to conceal their sites by lying, covering their tracks. But most are happy to share the fruits of their labors, the fruited mushroom, the finished product, however fraught. You can share, without sharing everything.
- c) Decide you have worked too hard for this mushroom. It is too valuable to let go. THIS IS YOUR FUCKING MUSHROOM. Find a way to deal with the damage:
  1. Cut it out completely.
  2. Work around it. Convince yourself it will be altered in the shaping/cooking of it anyways. Keep what isn't too bad, what you can still use, what's of value. If you can deal with it, so can everyone else.
  3. Take a deep breath and swallow it whole, bugs and all.

* * *

But here's the thing. The lobster mushroom, the parasitic fungus, has a superpower: it infests mushrooms, matter otherwise inedible, possibly toxic, and makes it safe for consumption. Palatable. Even delicious.

* * *

Is this a craft essay infected by a lyric essay, or a lyric essay infected by a craft essay?

Success in Circuit: Lyric Essay as Labyrinth

On Lateral Moves: *Lyric*

with thanks to Karen Babine for delightful turnings

Not a maze: "These casual observers never notice that the maze Lyric Essay has worn in the grass is a labyrinthine path; they never notice that the Lyric Essay's wanderings are structuring a carefully crafted border" (Wilson 2015).

But amazing: "We create passages for a reader to move through, seeing and sensing what we devise on the way. And when the reader's done—levitation! She looks down and sees how she's traveled, sees the pattern of the whole" (Alison 2019).

My first experience of a labyrinth was the movie with that name, one I watched repeatedly on a nascent HBO, a beautiful and disturbing fairy tale in which a nascent teen girl (Jennifer Connolly) must travel to the heart of the labyrinth to retrieve her infant brother from the Goblin King (a provocatively dressed David Bowie). Of course, that labyrinth was a maze. Or maybe not.

But currently, I'm in a bee-filled garden, drinking ice-cold cider and buzzing with Karen among piles of books. We're spending a summer afternoon talking around and around the issue of mode—what it is and how it affects movement—specifically, momentum in the lyric essay, what drives it forward so you end in a different place than you begin. I'm trying to articulate how—rather than a piece advancing by plot, with narrative/story moving us forward—and instead of logic advancing the argument of a piece—there are essays that are circuitous, nonlinear, that spiral around a central concept or incident or image, accruing meaning as they move. No forks, no false moves, no misdirection, only perhaps a pleasant disorientation as the writing twists and turns. It occurs to me such an essay might be described as a labyrinth. *To turn, turn will be our delight / Till by turning, turning we come round right.* Like Daedalus we construct both the meander as well as the thread to follow it, disorientation by design.

When I think of the labyrinth, aside from Bowie, I think of Borges, a master of the lyric essay, though I don't want to evoke the *Garden of Forking Paths*. While many conflate a labyrinth with a maze, they are not the same thing, and I want to amaze but not lose you. A maze is a puzzle that puts all choices of path and direction with the walker. There are many dead ends. In a labyrinth, the only choice is whether to enter. A labyrinth is defined by its circuits, its singular/unicursal path solved merely by walking. The way in is the way out, a *via negativa*.

If this were a maze, we would need Ariadne's *clew*—a ball of thread and the source of our word *clue*—to follow. But this is a labyrinth, and if the way in is the way out is the way through, then in a well-constructed lyric essay, we don't need a clue. Or, rather, the path *is* the clew, the thread unspooling. When I say "thread," it is important to remember that while Daedalus designed the walls defining the structure, it is the path—the white space, the *via negativa*—that gives a labyrinth its capability, an artistic space to move through, to engage with—both the literal white space employed in fragmented lyric essays and the figurative white spaces, the lyrical lateral leaps in logic across which we bound faithfully, propelled by the prose. *To turn, turn will be our delight.* This affinity for the lyric, for poetic prose, comes from its source in *verse*, which means *to turn*, its recursive language spiraling but not out of control. The careful writer keeps that path open, if not always apparent—an intention that can be traced, though not always at first reading. There will be clues. The author means to lead, not lose, you.

While the lyric essay may follow the labyrinth, Karen and I are prisoners in a maze, and our discussion resembles Borges's Garden, with forks we do not follow, false turns, retracing our steps. What is mode, and how is it different from form or shape? Is essay (noun) a form, but essay (verb) a mode? Does pure lyric exist in prose? Must there always be movement, and does it have to be forward? Can it be recursive so long as it's not redundant? Can I have another piece of rhubarb Bundt cake? Who's doing this well, and what do they call it? Who decides taxonomy—the writer or critical reader? But I have taken notes and am returned to tell you all.

Brian Doyle made a great Daedalus and would concur that by turning, turning we come round right. Karen and I are now discussing his "Joyas Voladoras" (Doyle 2019, 3–5), how it's not linear but has a path through it. Labyrinthine. I am reminded there's a moment as you near the center of the labyrinth where you turn, are turned, back—sent spiraling to the outer circuits, left wondering if you've lost the thread, clueless. In his essay, we start with the speed of a hummingbird's heart, its beauty giving way to its brief beating. Then we move sideways, turn toward consideration of other hearts—those of whales and birds and worms—before eventually wending to the human. In verse, in poetry, there is a term for a rhetorical turn called the *volta*. Just before the heart of this circuitous essay that beats so bright and briefly, we reverse course and zoom out, turn back to human scenes which seem unrelated, before, like a thousand volts, we are sent straight to the heart of the essay, the labyrinth's center. But Doyle has prepared us, unspooling that thread throughout for us to follow across the white space of his paragraph breaks and subject leaps, an intention that can be traced.

There must be a path to follow, a negative capability inherent in the design. When I was a young, inexperienced artist, I got the Chartres labyrinth, a cathedral floor design, tattooed on my back by a similarly young, inexperienced Daedalus. Tattoos, like lyric essays, are best crafted by someone with control of its elements, someone who can balance intuition with technique, lest the structure collapses. While I loved the experience of getting that tattoo—the meditative humming as the stylus traced its design in black ink—and while I loved the tattoo at first, twenty years later it has turned into a muddy mess—identifiable, but the path is gone, the thread lost. Recently, I went to a consultation for a new tattoo, the new artist and I again each of a similar age but now with the skill of years of practice. After we settled on the new image and its placement, talk turned to my other tattoos. It made her sad that I hated my labyrinth tattoo, though she was not responsible. She offered to fix it, not by re-inking the labyrinth, as I assumed, but rather the inverse: to trace its obscured path, what makes the pattern possible to traverse, in white ink, redefining and reclaiming it. Her stylus would emphasize that white space, that *via negativa*, so I could feel positive about the tattoo once again. Her turning would be my delight, her intention traced in white. Talking about Doyle's essay reminds me of my appointment, and when I tell Karen about this revelation, this revolution, she says, *you have to write this essay.*

When I do so, when I turn to research, I find a darker metaphor for the labyrinth's path is Christ's Harrowing of Hell, symbolic of him breaking death's prison. This, in turn, is reinterpreted as the Road to Jerusalem, inscribed in medieval cathedrals like Chartres, a substitute for those pilgrims who would walk Christ's path but could not make the trip. Either way, the labyrinth is reenacted as a journey inward, through physical and metaphysical space, in order to return transformed.

At the end of *Labyrinth*, the girl Sarah meets the Goblin King at the center and solves his puzzle by declaring "You have no power over me." This might suggest that the maze maker possesses no real power, that it's all a lovely fraud. What it actually reveals is that this maze was, in fact, a labyrinth: its process was not the physical path but an interior journey that leads Sarah to this realization.

But that space must be meaningful—you want the reader to be a willing pilgrim within its patterns, not a prisoner—otherwise they might strike across the floor's pattern, fly away, escape. Like a literary Lazarus, an undead Daedalus, I am returned to tell you all the clew to the lyric essay: a labyrinth using its repetitions with variations, its circuitous patterning, to delight and disorient but lead us, turning and leaping, in its ritual dance around its center.

A Jump to the Left, and Then a Step to the Right: On Lateral Moves in the Lyric Essay

On Lateral Moves: Traditional

In my lyric craft essay "Success in Circuit: The Lyric Essay as Labyrinth," I both describe and enact ways in which the lyric essay may turn itself without advancing, making sidestepping moves as it circles its subject, much like the circuitous path of a labyrinth. While that piece is presented as a lyric demonstration, I wanted to offer as a follow-up, a more straightforward explanation, with examples of these lateral moves. These moves include creating either parallels or reversals and spatial placements that may be either of those two.

And some terms: when I'm talking about mode—lyric, narrative, assay/meditative, didactic—I'm referencing both classical applications (cf. Aristotle on lyric versus narrative, dramatic, didactic) and the more current taxonomy offered for discussion by Karen Babine at *LitHub* (Babine 2020), the result of several conversations as she worked through her ideas. (In a nutshell, Babine subdivides literary nonfiction into genre, subgenre, form, mode, and shape in order to start a conversation—not on rigid classifications but to describe what a piece is doing.) While I am primarily interested in and focused on the lyric essay, these moves can be used in other nonfiction essay modes. In particular, lateral moves are used for pacing and to create suspense in the narrative mode. In assay/meditative mode, lateral moves incorporate history or research, offer or explore alternatives in the process of the author thinking through a topic or problem, what Judith Kitchen calls "digressions" in her essay "The Art of Digression" (Kitchen 2012), where she describes some of the same techniques I'll discuss below. But while the lateral moves I'll be describing can occur in other essay modes, I'd argue they tend to appear in greater density in lyric mode: so many of the moves are based in language and, on the page (especially since the early twentieth century), with language's relationship to space (arrangement, breaks, white space). This makes sense, since language and its music are the primary interest of pure lyricism. Here, I have great respect for Katharine Coles, who puts it best in her critical essay "If a Body" fleshed out from a brilliant panel presentation she made at NonfictioNOW's 2018 conference. She explains, "I use 'lyric' as a noun differently than I do 'lyric' as an adjective, where for me it indicates a reliance on dense musicality and imagery." She goes on to clarify the difference, for her, between narrative and lyric: "narrative works operate structurally through narrative gesture, the 'if/then' movement of cause and effect, about which lyric cares not. The pure lyric may gesture or hint at narrative possibility, which it nonetheless sequesters *outside* itself, operating instead through the this-and simultaneity we recognize in metaphor and metonymy, which purports to move us along while still keeping us from getting anywhere" (Coles 2019). While Coles's piece does important work demonstrating how the lyric can bridge poetry and prose, I disagree slightly with her description of pure lyric as lack of movement. Rather, I argue there is *lateral* movement, a resistance or delay to forward movement in the "this-and" Coles cites, which nonetheless moves us through the lyric essay.

But it's also important here to distinguish the ways in which the movement and handling of time in the lyric (and therefore in lyric essays) are more fluid than in other modes, which makes these lateral moves so prominent. Carl Dennis, in "The Temporal Lyric," describes the two "plots" of lyric poetry as the temporal—"a psychological development in which the speaker reaches a position by the end of the poem different from the one he or she occupies in the beginning"—and the nontemporal, which involves "the amplification and intensification of a single state of mind" (Dennis 2008, 236). In both cases, the lyric may resist forward movement, so long as the piece brings the reader to a new position or richer understanding. Heather McHugh, in "Moving Means, Meaning

Moves: Notes on Lyric Destination," argues "A poem means to move you, but in unexpected directions. . . . In poems, the convention of continuance is always being queried by poetic structure. . . . It is a structure of internal resistances" (McHugh 1996, 208). Here, she refers to the ways in which the poem's forward movement is constantly in tension with the arrangement of its language on the page, across lines, breaks, and space. But because the lyric essay employs many of the same disjunctions, an examination of how these poetic structures function or are adapted in prose is important. To create lyric tension, the lyric essay may also resist forward movement, instead moving laterally. These moves include creating either parallels or reversals, and spatial placements that may be either of those two.

The first group of lateral moves are those that create parallels—"this-and"—placing similar elements in apposition. These include images, scenes, or situations resonating with each other, placed in proximity to heighten and call attention to those resonances. Nicole Walker's "Fish" is a triptych in three different writing styles, scenes, and points of view—nature documentary/lyric, memoir, and food writing—and each section presents only a brief, image-based moment addressing some aspect of fish. While each section has its distinct voice, images and words echo across the essay: the straining of the salmon upstream becomes the straining of the young girl and barracuda against each other, and returns as directions for making a sauce: "Strain through a chinois. Strain through cheese cloth. Strain one more time for good measure" (Walker 2013, 1). Words like "circling," "hold," and "flesh" recur, accruing meaning—Dennis's nontemporal "amplification and intensification of a single state of mind." Eula Biss's fragmentary essay "Time and Distance Overcome" juxtaposes scenes of telephone poles linked to violence to complicate the ideas of connection and division at the birth of telephony, the resistance to forward movement mimicking resistance to (and, in the case of racism, a lack of) progress (Biss 2008).

The parallel move also may be achieved via language, especially in lyric essays. One way to accomplish this is by exploring the etymology of a word to discover or create links between two ideas. Sun Yung Shin's "The Hospitality of Strangers," in her excellent lyric collage *Unbearable Splendor* on her transnational and transracial adoption (a book which happens to have a labyrinth on its cover!), traces the sources and cognates of the Old English *gest*, which means both guest and stranger and is related to the words host, hostile, and hospitality, in order to interrogate borders and immigration (Shin 2016, 13–16). The author might employ wordplay, invoking a similar-sounding word to suggest a linkage or slide the meaning from one word to a seemingly unrelated one. I've done this myself in a lyric essay "Cuir," where I recount the entwined history of leather and perfume: "from *cuir* to *queer*, the veneer of sweat-stained chaps and battered motorcycle jackets, leather's skin-on-skin action" (Czerwiec 2019, 13). In "Dee Aster," one of the section-starting pieces Lee Ann Roripaugh calls "language betrayals" from her remarkable collection *Dandarians*, she moves from "disaster" to her mispronunciation "Dee Aster," which gets her to the traumas of "Lee Aster" (Roripaugh 2014, 57–60). Maybe my initial assertion of "creates links" is incorrect: in using this technique, the author doesn't exactly create connections so much as reveals them, the trace of the author made visible.

The author might also signal more clearly she's creating a parallel through such phrase tags as "at the same time" or "at that time" to parallel two simultaneously occurring events, or by saying "that reminds me of" or "which makes me think of" to suggest a connection which exists only because of the author's process of mind or stream of consciousness. At the beginning of Terese Mailhot's *Heart Berries*, her lyric account of trauma, mental illness, and reconciliation, she says, "I knew I was not well. I thought of the first healer, who was just a boy. My friend Denise told me the story. She called him Heart Berry Boy, or O'dimin.... The people in his village were sick and dying because the Indian world was shifting" (Mailhot 2018, 12–13). She then relates the tale of the first medicine, wild strawberries, and the first medicine man of the people. This "field of concurrent times" links Mailhot both to original trauma and to potential healing. This requires a bit more explanation of lyric time and how it differs from narrative time. Time in poetry includes the tension between its progress and its structures of internal resistance, but there's more to it. *Radiant Lyre*, an anthology of craft essays on lyric poetry, includes marvelous critical work on lyric time. In "To Think of Time," David Baker says,

Poetry is about the varieties of measuring, telling, and thinking about time.... The interesting question is not *whether* a poem has a story in it, but rather *what kind* of time-telling the poem undertakes. Time may be suppressed, elongated, distorted, or abbreviated. It may be spotty, circular, or linear. It may, as in a palimpsest or a bad photograph, be multiply exposed. Time may be a field of concurrent times.

(Baker 2007, 242)

This seems to be a revision of Dennis's nontemporal amplification—here, rather, we have multitemporal amplification, what Stanley Plumly in "Lyric Time" describes as "those concerns in present time amplified, compared, and analogized in past time—the moment juxtaposed with mythic memory" (Baker 2007, 265–6). In these lateral moves created by paralleling events or moments, lyric time is shown to its greatest effect.

The second group of lateral moves involves opposition rather than apposition—"this-but" rather than "this-and"—reversals, or at least restarts that don't move the piece forward (or don't immediately seem to), but rather move in an opposite or new direction. This might be done using anaphora, a technique where an initial word or phrase is repeated at the start of each line or paragraph, acting as a reset button or a listing mechanism, as in John Scalzi's "Being Poor," which is a list of details from shifting perspectives (old, young, parent, woman), all of which begin "Being poor is" to create a composite portrait of poverty (Scalzi 2005). This could also be signaled with phrase tags, such as "or, rather," "not *x*, but *y*," or some negation that refutes what came before in favor of what is now being offered, or at least offers alternatives. I do this in "Consider the Lobster Mushroom," when I compare writing nonfiction to the lobster mushroom, which is actually a mushroom infected with a parasitic fungus:

> You become infected by an idea, a topic . . . that absorbs you, imparting its own qualities, until you're transformed, not the same person as before. // Or, you may play the part of parasite—cloak your work, make it take the appearance of another form.... // Or, you may think you're writing one essay, but another essay takes it over, makes it its own.

This kind of move could also be presented via revision, such as redoing a scene in a different way by changing point of view, or even "perhapsing" an imagined alternate scene (a useful term proffered by Lisa Knopp), as Anika Fajardo does in "What Didn't Happen" when she imagines an alternate unlived life (Fajardo 2014), or at the level of language by saying something again but using a different tone, register, or rhythm. Dinah Lenney does this in her "Little Black Dress," where each paragraph starts with a new shift in the speaker's register, from lofty to blunt to wistful: "O, you should be able to say when you bought this dress and what for." "So. Is it actually, finally time to retire the little black dress?" "You remember a dinner party in Laurel Canyon" (Lenney 2017). In presenting these alternatives—logical, thematic, emotional, tonal—the lyric essay explodes with multiple possibilities, creating a density of intended meanings within a compressed space.

The final group of lateral moves is more ambiguous and spatial, and involves juxtaposing and/or braiding items/fragments across white space. The author lays down one thread in order to pick up another, signaling this with white space. White space is one poetry technique which has received some nonfiction craft attention—I am reminded especially of Dinty W. Moore, Robert Root, Amy Bonnaffons, and others I cover more extensively in my essay on white space, "Negative Capability." In any case, for white space as a lateral move, it's left more to the reader to determine whether the fragments are being placed in apposition, opposition, or something else. To return to a previous example, the fragments of Eula Biss's "Time and Distance Overcome" function like telephone poles, stringing their connections across the dividing white space—what is communicated? There may be no clear sense of accrual, however, and the effect may be jarring. Here, I think especially of Kathy Fish's flash piece "Collective Nouns for Humans in the Wild," with its startling catalogue of proposed names for groups that culminates in a gutpunch of a shift at the end. In fact, in this example, it's the white space that creates the gutpunch, with its pacing, pause, and then succinct, deadly delivery (Fish 2017). (I don't want to ruin it for those of you who haven't read it—it's quite short and available online, so you should look it up now; the URL is available in the Suggested Readings at the end of this book.)

But an essay, even a quite lyric or fragmented essay, cannot succeed solely through lateral moves or leaps. At some point or points, the piece needs to advance in order to develop or arrive at a revelation, however small. Inexperienced writers experimenting with the form sometimes attempt to move only by juxtaposition, fragments laid down, a series of "this-ands" without a sense of accrual or summation, and it ends up feeling static and flat. Here, I find it especially useful to apply what's called "bound association," by way of Eula Biss: in a Q&A at a recent reading by Biss, she cited poet Robyn Schiff, who distinguishes between "free association" and "bound association." In the latter, Schiff explains how you bind yourself only to the trajectory of certain terms, to keep yourself from pursuing infinite rabbit holes. Biss went on to say that when using this process, she goes back and tries to figure out how she got from one leap to the next, to fill in any gaps, while also trying to preserve wonder (Biss 2020). I really like this for a summation: the lyric essay may move laterally through the various associative techniques I've outlined, but there are limits and bounds, and needs to be a trajectory, a path that, ultimately, leads us to wonder.

Lyric Time

As Jane Alison of *Meander, Spiral, Explode* explains it, when we write, we "can hold a reader fixed, making her feel not her own time, but the time we devise" (Alison 2019, 44–5). We're more conscious of time in narrative work and often expect it to be manipulated in certain prescribed ways in stories, memoirs, and essays: starting *in medias res*; slowing down with scene, dialogue, or description; or possibly telling events out of order, though in such a way that the "master" narrative or chronology can be pieced together. However, as poet-critic Ellen Bryant Voigt points out, a straightforward narrative is itself a manipulation: because narrative linearity or through-lines are only true in retrospect, that makes "narrative, with its allegiance to sequence and continuity, with its illusion of significance and order, as much a manipulation of experience as the lyric's isolation and examination of moments of extreme emotional dilemma" (Voigt 1999, 109–10). This supposed "sequence and continuity" and "illusion of significance and order" would be equally true of essays in assay mode as well, which create the effect of a thread of coherent thought only after the mind is done wandering.

We assume that in the lyric, with its focus on the moment, time isn't such a factor, but inversely it is, via its disruption in the tension created between its progress and its structures of internal resistance. As I'll make clear later, critics often incorrectly describe the lyric or lyric essay as "nonlinear" or "disjunctive," despite how they do create junctions/connections in other ways, sonically and imagistically. But by nonlinear or disjunctive, what critics mean is this way in which the lyric disrupts time. With lyric strategies, time can be manipulated, disrupted, or even stopped. As a result, it's more accurate to consider the quality of time in a piece, how overtly it's manipulated or disrupted in ways that have nothing to do with narrative. In "To Think of Time," poet and critic David Baker delineates the nonlinear beautifully:

> Poetry is about the varieties of measuring, telling, and thinking about time. . . . The interesting question is not *whether* a poem has a story in it, but rather *what kind* of time-telling the poem undertakes. Time may be suppressed, elongated, distorted, or abbreviated. It may be spotty, circular, or linear. It may, as in a palimpsest or a bad photograph, be multiply exposed. Time may be a field of concurrent times.

Linearity is an illusion in any mode, but what makes lyric time functionally lyric are the non-narrative strategies deployed: "Poetry wishes to defray the damages of the inexorable, or at least to clarify and perhaps to exploit them; to accomplish this, poetry proposes alternate methods of making and keeping time." Baker says these strategies include meter (which in the lyric essay could be alternatively termed "cadence"; see "Strike a Chord"), grammar and syntax (see "Structures of Thinking"), and other poetic effects like line and line break (see "Negative Capability" on white space and fragments), caesuras and hyphens (see "A Dash of Dash"), heavy or quickened syllables (see "Strike a Chord"), or compression/density/ambiguity of meaning (see "Structures of Thinking") (Baker 2007, 242–4).

Therefore, lyric time may involve manipulation/distortion of time, multiple times represented either juxtaposed or else superimposed as if concurrently, or stopped/disrupted—and, I would argue, these strategies are deployed equally in the lyric essay as in the poem.

The first way a lyric essay progresses through time lyrically, and not based on narrative/linear time, may be to represent the process of mind, following a deepening or train of thought—a dilation, distortion, or manipulation of time that mimics the way the author's mind wanders, pauses, obsesses over something, connects it to something else. As Carl Dennis puts it in "The Temporal Lyric,"

> Although we often contrast the lyric with the narrative poem, within the lyric itself one may distinguish two kinds of structure, one temporal, one not. Both kinds of poems may be said to

be plotted, with a rationale for the sequence of parts, but the nontemporal plot involves the amplification and intensification of a single state of mind while the temporal plot presents a psychological development in which the speaker reaches a position by the end of the poem different from the one he or she occupies in the beginning.

(Dennis 2008, 236)

This could include some of the strategies I describe in "Image Alt-Narratives" (deepening or tracing an image) and "Strike a Chord" (use of sonic effects), where what Baker says about compression/density/ambiguity of meaning as well as cadence and heavy syllables could be used to slow down, deepen, elongate, or distort time, while quickened cadence or syllables and refrain and syntax could be used to show development.

For instance, I discuss in "Image Alt-Narratives" how Brian Doyle pushes in on the "hand in hand" image of a couple jumping from one of the Towers in his brief essay on 9/11, "Leap." But he couples the recurrence of this image with sonic syntactical effects, alternating long, discursive sentences with terse, matter-of-fact witness accounts all beginning, "[X] saw...." By employing both rushing syntax and constant hard reset-buttons of anaphora, along with the repetitions of image, Doyle tries to sustain a single moment—the couple leaping hand in hand—suspending them indefinitely in an attempt to delay the inevitable (Doyle 2003, 129–31).

These developments could also take various nonlinear shapes. Jane Alison's *Meander, Spiral, Explode* describes alternatives to the traditional arc or pyramid of narrative development, and as a result, her book has been embraced by creative nonfiction writers also exploring alternative structures. In the following quote from Alison, I've replaced "story" or "narrative" with "essay" or "lyric essay":

> All of these different approaches can be seen within the larger scheme of natural patterns. What seems to be the generative impulse or starting point for a [lyric essay]; how does it move in time; how does it employ repetition? A digressive [essay] meanders; at times it flows quickly and at times barely at all, often loops back on itself, yet ultimately it moves onward. A

spiraling [essay] might move around and around with a system of rhythmic repetitions, yet it advances, deepening into the past, perhaps, or rising into the future. . . . A fractal [essay] could branch from a core or seed, repeating at different scales the shape or dynamic of that core, possibly branching on indefinitely.

(Alison 2019, 23)

To make such essays lyric, the digressive meander could manipulate time as described in the previous paragraph, while the spiral or fractal could repeat and/or vary patterns of sound, image, or syntax. In fact, the lateral moves I describe in "A Jump to the Left. . ." can also be used to manipulate the progression of time.

Essays using the strategy of lyric time demonstrate how time may not follow a chronological, linear, cause-and-effect sequence of events, but rather take a particular moment or event and use shape (spiral, fractal) to show how that moment echoes (spirals, ripples, fractals) outward, repeating itself in patterns of behavior. This is evident in the two hybrid memoirs below.

Sheila O'Connor's *Evidence of V* is a fragmentary history filled in with imagined scenes of her maternal grandmother unconstitutionally incarcerated in a Minnesota facility for "immoral" girls as a teen pregnant with O'Connor's mother and is also a collage of epigenetic trauma that follows. The wrongful incarceration of V, with its fragmentary case file simultaneously official record and erasure, becomes the black hole around which O'Connor's text spirals as she constantly interrupts the narrative to muse on its meaning, as well as the main trunk of the fractal branching through the biological family. In the opening "First the facts" section, the listing of who/what/where/when/why disrupts the historical narrative to list its elements, demonstrating instead how the author connects them. Under "WHO" is listed

> V, mother of my mother. Absent and erased. V, maternal grandmother. Both missing and maternal?
> Mr. C, maternal grandfather?
> June, born of V and Mr. C
> June, my mother not maternally inclined (O'Connor 2019, 5)

where the format and repetitions create a pattern, and the various meanings of "maternal" create both a density and complicated ambiguity of meaning. "WHEN" displays the time frame of the research, yet asserts that the story begun in 1935 is ongoing "ad infinitum": "The length of time V's cells transmit her trauma to us all: June's children, and our children, and—   As in today: Call sibling in the psych ward" (O'Connor 2019, 5), all that time compressed into a brief, branching list connecting V's incarceration to the author's institutionalized brother.

Similarly, Marco Wilkinson's lyric memoir *Madder: A Memoir in Weeds* expands out fractally, growing like the family trees and dissemination of weeds and wild plants he parallels both in text and incorporated visual elements, all linked to a heritage of gardening and stemming from a lie about his parentage. In the opening essay "Weeds, A Semblance," he repeats the refrain "I am a gardener" like the women of his mother's family, yet identifies himself with weeds, also refrained with "A weed is":

> A weed is excessive, too good for its own or anyone else's good. . . . An overachiever, it surprises and perplexes when so little was asked of it. // A weed is out of place. . . . // A weed is no use for one who has no use for it. . . . I will burn up this uselessness— what my family used to call me my whole childhood, *inútil*. I will burn up this uselessness to keep warm. I will burn up this uselessness to tell a story by, until the world around me catches fire. I will burn up this uselessness until this uselessness has had done with the useful.
> (Wilkinson 2021, 4–6)

And yet, though he feels like the seed of this family disruption, we discover it is his mother's seminal lie about his origins that both branches outward in time toward the author's present-day, but also backward through his family roots.

Another manipulation or disruption of time might involve representing multiple points in time—past, present, future, imagined, and mythic—and either moving between them or creating a palimpsest where the times all occur concurrently. In referring to Baker's list of lyric strategies, this representation of multiple times could be evoked through compression of image or language across time periods, ambiguities that allow them to run together, and/or line and line breaks that might translate to the white spaces of fragmentation. Stanley Plumly's "Lyric Time" describes how this happens in poetry: in Keats's nightingale ode, "those concerns in present time [are] amplified, compared, and analogized in past time—the moment juxtaposed with mythic memory," while Whitman's long "Crossing Brooklyn Ferry" "give[s] him a good deal of room in which to muse, repeat, speculate, commiserate, observe, record, and travel in his mind between past and future, life and afterlife, here and now and when" (Baker 2007, 265–7).

In the lyric essay, in order to heighten the sense of conflating and creating ambiguity between different moments in time, they might be run together with no breaks in the text and with refrains of sound and/or imagery, as seen in Diane Seuss's [I hoisted them, two drug dealers], when the events of the mother throwing out the drug dealers preying on her son, giving birth to her son by C-section, and fighting with her addict son all inhabit the same brief space and single sentence (Seuss 2021a, 67).

Or the multiple points or events in time might be separated by white space, at which point the reader must decide how the sections or fragments relate, which I detail in "Negative Capability." As Alison explains in one of her patterns, "cellular narratives come in like parts, not moving forward in time from one to another but creating a network of meaning" (Alison 2019, 23). In fact, in the lyric essay, this use of white space replaces the loss of the poetic line break's disruption, helping the reader to continue to chunk meaning, while still requiring the reader to read into those spaces. Again, Alison: "A pool of white surrounding a raft of words rests the eye and creates the time-space for a reader to draw connections or ponder" (Alison 2019, 37). The result is a space that requires readers to ask the following questions: Are those multiple times being connected, contrasted, or merely considered side-by-side? And what do the relations between the parts, and the use of white space, mean?

Mary Ruefle's "*My* Emily Dickinson," collected in *Madness, Rack, and Honey*, starts from the proposition "I decided to write a lecture called 'My Emily Dickinson,'" which immediately gets bound up with time-conflating considerations of Emily Brontë and Anne Frank and her own writing:

> The next afternoon I happened upon a sidewalk sale of books, and there, gleaming up at me, gleaming and reaching, reaching and gleaming, speaking to me, speaking to me in a voice I barely recognized at first, because it was not a voice I knew, because it was a voice I had loved well but long ago, because it was my own voice all entwined with another's, was a voice telling me to pick up the book and start reading. And it was like learning to read all over again. And it was poetry. And it was Emily Brontë.
>
> (Ruefle 2012, 145)

The rest of the lecture moves through various topics in set-off sections, juxtaposing separate paragraphs that compare and contrast and sometimes conflate these writers' lives. Under "Living Conditions": "Emily Dickinson never lived alone for a single day of her life"; "Emily Brontë never lived alone for a single day of her life"; "Anne Frank was a gregarious and popular girl who was housebound the last two years of her life" (147–8). Ruefle ends this section "Emily and Emily both lived in houses with views of a graveyard. Anne, at the end of her life, lived *in* a graveyard" (149). Ruefle seems to be thinking through the issue of connection alongside the reader: "I don't know if there is a connection. If Anne the young writer had lived, I think she would have wondered the same thing—if there was a connection. Clearly Emily lived long enough to wonder if there was a connection. Sometimes we wonder if there is a connection. And sometimes we know there is no connection, but we wonder then if one might be possible. It is all very confusing, to say the least" (177). These "cellular" considerations of women writers create connections, combine to form a whole beyond the parts: Emilys who expand to include an Anne until the whole comprises not Emily Dickinson but "*My* Emily Dickinson," a creation made of wonder via connection, a wonder she transfers to us.

Early in Claudia Rankine's *Citizen: An American Lyric* on the experience of race in America, she quotes Zora Neale Hurston— "I feel most colored when I am thrown against a sharp white background"—and uses the white space of the page to throw into relief the text where she relates these temporal moments of racist aggression, both micro- and macro-, both personal and historical. Each is experienced on its own page, each surrounded by white space, Alison's "pool of white" turned threat where Black people are made to feel most colored in the White spaces of society (Rankine 2014). (I describe one notable example in the "Unsaid" section of "Negative Capability.")

Lyric time may also be slowed to a stop, utterly disrupted, absorbed in an eternally present memory. Some of this is based in Romantic lyric theory: in "Genre Theory, the Lyric, and *Erlebnis*," René Wellek tells us:

> The crux of [Staiger's argument] lies in the coordination of the 'lyrical' with the 'past,' which seems to contradict all the usual analyses of lyrical presence or immediacy. But the Heideggerian use of 'Erinnerung' allows the term to mean a lack of distance between subject and object. . . . The time scheme is abolished for the lyrical mode, permitting gestures toward the mystical and ineffable.
>
> (Jackson and Prins 2014, 45)

Wellek also notes that both Humboldt and Schelling claim that the lyric belongs to an eternal present and that Vischer says, "in lyrical poetry everything becomes present in feeling" (48). In other words, the memory is only ever recalled and re-experienced in the present, creating an immediacy erasing any distance between subject and memory—and, in the lyric, erasing that distance for the reader experiencing it vicariously. Lyric strategies in the lyric essay reinforcing this include white space (again replacing line and line break) to reset or disrupt time, grammar and syntax (especially present verb tense and adjectives that slow down description), anaphora, slow cadence/heavy syllables and density/compression to slow down text. In "A Mind for Metaphors," Ann Townsend argues that this effect is profoundly lyrical: "Genuinely disinterested in narrative self-fashioning, Strawson believes instead that episodic personalities prefer to live more exclusively in the present tense. I'll leap here and suggest that an episodic frame of mind is also a lyric frame of mind. Reading a lyric poem, we experience an illusion of stopped time, of radical subjectivity" (Baker 2007, 231).

However, this stopping or disruption of time often is used in nonfiction to represent feeling trapped in a traumatic memory or event that feels eternally present. Lyric time and traumatic time feature many of the same techniques and qualities: forward progress disrupted by white space and/or fragmentation, and repetition or density of sound, image, and syntactical structures that keep us in a loop. Voigt recognizes this parallel: "Like trauma, lyric contradicts the linear—it 'stops time'—and to do so uses simultaneous, sometimes opposing perceptions, a dense fabric of emotive language, highly musical arrangements of texture, and alternative organizations of those arrangements" (Voigt 1999, 135). And Alison seems to describe this time loop when she suggests, "A radial narrative could spring from a central hole—an incident, pain, absence, horror—around which it keeps circling or from which it keeps veering, but it scarcely moves forward in time" (Alison 2019, 23).

Theresa Cha describes, or rather enacts, this eternally present trauma-loop in *Dictee*, a hybrid (auto)biography of several women, most notably her mother, whose Korean family is violently uprooted. To do so, she effectively uses these strategies of fragmented sentences and repetition and verb choices to create a "dense fabric of emotive language" that arrests all movement, collapsing past, present, future, and even future perfect into the author's present:

> Mother, you are eighteen years old. You were born in Yong Jung, Manchuria and this is where you now live. You are not Chinese. You are Korean. But your family moved here to escape the Japanese occupation. . . . You live in a village where the other Koreans live. Same as you. Refugees. Immigrants. Exiles. Farther away from the land that is not your own. Not your own any longer.
>
> You did not want to see. You cannot see anymore. What they do. To the land and to the people. As long as the land is not your own. Until it will be again. Your father left and your mother left as the others. You suffer the knowledge of having to leave. Of having left. But your MAH-UHM, spirit has not left. Never shall have and never shall will. Not now. Not even now. It is burned into your ever-present memory. Memory less. Because it is not in the past. It cannot be. Not in the least of all pasts.
>
> (Cha 2001, 45)

To conclude, I also want to point to another variable in lyric time: the time, or times, experienced by the reader. Stanley Plumly lists these various experiences of time in his "Lyric Time":

> Time, for instance, as a measure within and without the poem: that is, the conceit of the amount of time implied or covered within the 'action' of the poem; the actual time the poem takes, say sonnet-time as opposed to fifty or eighty lines of the hundred-and-thirty-two lines required to cross the East River from Manhattan to Brooklyn; or timing time, the rhythm, the cadence, the metrical time, the length-of-line time across then down the page, pacing time. Then there is the time *after* the poem, relative to its displacement, density, and resonance, the reading and reflective time, the breadth of time necessary to absorb the time of and with a lyric poem.
>
> (Baker 2007, 264)

In terms of the lyric essay, a short but densely resonant and heavily stressed paragraph like Cha's might take us much more time to read and parse and then comprehend; Seuss's prose sonnet of the same length rushes us through its single sentence so rapidly that after its initial force and thrill we must return and re-read it for its nuances. A segmented essay with lots of white space, like Ruefle's or O'Connor's or Rankine's, forces me to pause and try to discern how the pieces relate. Or, the beauty of the language or intensity of thought might strike me so hard I have to stop and stare out the window a while. And here I am, much later, and these examples continue to echo in my head.

Mind the Gap: Writing Around Absence

On Uses of Space: *Lyric*

4.

Perhaps because memories are full of gaps. Perhaps because research is also full of gaps, and it's the gaps that are interesting. So many gaps, a painful mouth, the tongue keeps tonguing. *La langue.* A structure poststructuralists say has no center, an absent heart.

Where is the heart? I imagine it gone wandering around in its own body, how the womb was once thought to. Perhaps the heart imagines a new story for itself with perhapsing (Knopp 2009), filling its space with words, making a myth it is the hero of. I like to picture it off to the side of the official record of the known world, studying the marginalia, using it as a springboard to dive into another, if not several, alternate possibilities. In researching so-called "witches," women's knowledge and persecution for it, Kathryn Nuernberger admits in *The Witch of Eye*, "I might have fallen in love, I might have been burned, I might have given up the name of my own dear friend, I might have set the hour of execution, might have pulled the fingernails, might have set the pins, might have been pregnant, might have lost my child, I might have looked around at all I owned and wondered how I could ever hold on to it all" (Nuernberger 2021, 86). The way Elissa Washuta projects herself through her psychiatrist's eyes in "Note" from *My Body Is a Book of Rules*, a record of her treatment in fairly clinical language, but which also includes such nuggets as "I disclosed to the patient that she was my favorite patient," "I missed her a lot when she left," and "If anyone. . .tells her to shrug it off and cheer up, I have promised her I will personally kick his or her teeth in," and concludes with the endnote "With edits from Elissa Washuta" (Washuta 2014, 9–14). How Sheila O'Connor composes a composite biological grandmother from scraps of records of teenaged birthmothers to assemble *Evidence of V*, which opens with a bracketed aside:

> [. . .
> . . .
>
> Shhh.   The sound of V is silence.
>
> Girl of sealed history like all those other girls.
> Sealed; therefore buried.
>
> State documents I now excavate for answers.
> An official file of facts that read like fiction.
>
> V a fiction built of fragments, as girls so often are.]
>
> (O'Connor 2019, 1, ellipses mine)

I like to imagine all that imagining and perhapsing embroidering that gap until it doesn't feel so empty, possibly beautiful.

3.

It's the solving for X, not X itself, that matters. X has a value, even if that value remains unknown. Every solution a new possibility. An equation moves through the process of not-knowing, via the partially known, the half-grasped, ever elusive.

X is an elegant concept. But how will it help me in real life? In stories of real life? Math is stupid. Just give me the answer. Why do I need to find X? Why does it matter so much? Not because of what X might equal, but because the searching might make the ghostly vessel of Doireann Ní Ghríofa's *a ghost in the throat*, keening widow-mother Eibhlín Dubh Ní Chonaill—might make herself, vessel of history, milk, and motherhood—more visible (Ní Ghríofa 2020). The equation at the heart of Carmen Machado's fragmentary memoir in flash, *In the Dream House*, each fragment titled "*Dream House* as [X]" (brackets mine), where the various substitutions for X reveal a new aspect of the abusive relationship: "*Dream House* as Erotica," "*Dream House* as Omen," "*Dream House* as Soap Opera," and so on (Machado 2019).

The writers I list here have an X chromosome, most XX. Not XXX, though, which suggests something forbidden, poisonous, that will leave your eyes x'ed out.

When you make your body into an X in yoga, stretching your arms and legs, the shape is called star, and the elusive X is the star here, generating the heat and energy to power the piece, even as all that potential energy has a black hole for a heart, the not-knowing a delicious suspension until it collapses on itself.

X the star shooting through the story as we search for it, search for meaning in our stars, even as the stars cross us.

2.

I erase the previous class's equations from the white board when I teach. Of course, wiping away can create its ghost, negative capability, a negative space not necessarily to be filled, but to be represented. Absence a presence defined by not-ness.

In *Dictee*, Therese Hak Kyung Cha represents the intergenerational traumas of Korean women, with a slippery "she" that at times represents various martyrs—Catholic and Korean—as well as her own mother:

> She forgets. She tries to forget. For the moment. For the duration of these moments.

> She opens the cloth again. White. Whitest of beige. In the whiteness, subtle hues outlining phoenix from below phoenix from above facing each other in the weave barely appearing. Disappearing into the whiteness.
> (Cha 2001, 113)

But do such erasures really disappear? I don't know. No one knew. We couldn't say. They never spoke about it.

[star wipe]

1.

Emily Dickinson knew something about—holding space—the power dashes have—

The white spaces hold so much—the ghost of her white dress—posing in the corner. They may be silent—but are not empty.

Like musical rests, like caesuras—which have value—as Robert Root asserts, this is what the spaces say (Root 2001).

John Cage experimented with silence in his music, after an experience in a completely soundproofed chamber—he realized that, far from silent, he could still hear his nervous and circulatory systems, his breath, a white noise.

Silence is impossibility.

Cage claimed he composed all the notes to *4'33"*—also called the "Silent Sonata"—but they were all silent (Cage 1959).

I think about this, reading Jenny Boully's *The Body: An Essay*, where the footnotes refer to a text that exists, fully imagined, but rendered unreadable, absent (Boully 2002).

Each note, each sound, each correspondence whited out.

o

Kintsugi, or "golden joinery": the Japanese art of repairing broken pottery by adding powdered gold to the mending lacquer, thereby making the crazed space, the rupture, visible and even valued.

o

Lack and *lacuna*, unrelated at their source, yet the source for both is wanting.

○

A Humument has been ~~a work in progress since 1966 when artist Tom Phillips set~~ himself a task: ~~to~~ find a second-~~hand book for threepence~~ and alter ~~every page by painting, collage, and cut-up techniques~~ to create a~~n entirely~~ new ~~version~~ (Phillips 1980).

Mary Ruefle's *White*

                remains visible

                                          (Ruefle 2006)

Chelsea Biondolillo has a piece, "The Story You Never Tell," which is an essay largely obscured by iden███llow glimps███one of several visual essays in *The Skinned Bird* (Biondolillo 2019, 32–46).

$X \times 0 = 0$. Zero, the great eraser, the great erasure.

○

An erasure of this section so far:

Emily knew spaces hold value, experiment with experience, breath, sound, wanting. A task to create the visible, skinned.

○

Terry Tempest Williams, in *When Women Were Birds*, recounts how her dying mother left all her journals to be read only after the coming death. When Williams does, she finds all the journals are blank. At first, this revelation is confusing, even cruel. "But now, 25 years after I first opened the journals, I am finally able to think about what this emptiness means. . . . There is an art to writing, and it is not always disclosure" (Williams 2012, 182).

John Cage said "I have nothing to say and I am saying it" (Cage 1959).

Zero at the Bone.

0.

A cross-section of bone looks a bit like a Zero, and that ain't nothing. Neither is Zero, according to Pythagoras, who believed in only numbers whole, *rational*, which is to say, a *ratio*, a number expressed as a ratio of two other numbers. Zero is *irrational*. By this, he is taken to mean Zero cannot exist because you cannot have no value. But Zero isn't without value, as musical rests aren't without value. A whole rest holds a whole count, holds a hole in sound. Aristotle: "A whole is what has a beginning, middle, and end." In that case, 0 simultaneously possesses none of these, yet rotates perpetually through all three. "Nick Cave would like to remind you that zero is also a number" is what the liner notes to the *X-Files* soundtrack *Songs in the Key of X* say (Was 1996), yet the song he hid in Track 0 was unlistenable on many systems. If a track plays on a CD, but no CD player will let you hear it, does 0 make a sound? What the spaces say: a witch's testimony, an absent parent, a missing memory, an elusive sense of understanding, an erasure. Nothing is always something. Anything + 0 = itself, Zero rendered transparent, a screen, a scrim, mirror in an oval frame that frames you. Even—especially—Absolute Zero looms large—lineated space that holds space—0—a cross-section of bone, a phantom limb, limning the missing, like all these lines of writing.

Negative Capability

On Uses of Space: Traditional

Warning: I am about to fill 20+ pages discussing white space in nonfiction. I recognize the paradox; I acknowledge the folly. But considering the lack of space given to explaining how it functions in creative nonfiction—several craft books' worth of white space, in fact—the words are clearly needed. Therefore, I'm going to attempt to do so, to—as poet Li-Young Lee puts it—"[use] words to make the silence palpable" (Lee 2006, 122).

White space occurs throughout creative nonfiction, but because of white space's proximity to and association with poetry, it occurs in higher incidence in the lyric essay, which has been and will be my main focus here. White space is one poetry technique which actually has received some nonfiction craft attention. Robert Root writes beautifully on this topic in "This Is What the Spaces Say," comparing segmented essays to the movements of a concerto or to the multiple panels of medieval altarpieces:

> [T]he most significant change in the nature of nonfiction in our time has been the use of space as an element in composition. . . . Segmented essays—sometimes called collage essays or disjunctive essays or paratactic essays—depend on space, usually expressed as numbers or rows of asterisks or squiggly lines or white breaks in text, as a fundamental element of design and expression. Knowing what the spaces say is vital to understanding the nonfictionist's craft and appreciating the possibilities of this contemporary form.

He says this form helps the essayist and the reader get at the truth: "expect to know whatever this essay is about in the same way you know anything else, in fragments of certainty and segments of supposition, surrounded by gaps in your knowledge and borders of uncertainty." However, he attributes this technique to nonfictionists' need to grapple with the truth, since they cannot "settle for the fictionist's 'higher truth through fabrication'" because, as he says, "The issue of truth...seldom surfaces in other literary genres" (Root 2001). Apparently, poets are not to be credited with either truth or technique or with having written decisive work on this very issue, such as Jorie Graham's "Some Notes on Silence" (Graham 1984); his negation of poetic contribution is an erasure on par with the oeuvre of Mary Ruefle. At least Dinty W. Moore acknowledges this debt to poetics in his excellent "Positively Negative" in *Bending Genre*: he states, "[Poets have] been thinking of white space, negative space, the distance between thoughts and words, since the time they first took up the pen," before lamenting "prose writers...seldom if ever articulate how white space works. . . . We use it, certainly, but I very seldom find it discussed in craft books or writing classrooms" (Moore 2013, 182). Much discussion of white space tends to divert to discussions of fragmentation and its functions, rather than on how the white space in and of itself is functioning. In my attempt to do so, I would like to return to its discussion in poetic craft sources in order to recognize the use of white space as a technique, and how it is and/or may be applied to the lyric essay.

First, a thumbnail history. Although fragments appear throughout literature, the expansion of white space as a technique largely comes from two concurrent developments in literature at the end of the nineteenth and start of the twentieth centuries. First, the production of relatively inexpensive typewriters meant writers could treat the blank page as a visual field to be manipulated, populated with text in a particular, idiosyncratic way that could be specifically indicated to and reproduced by the publisher, as recounted by poet-critics Harvey Gross and Robert McDowell:

> [T]he typewriter exerted significant influences on modern writing, affecting the rhythms of modern prose. Certainly, the iconographic effects Cummings achieved with the distribution of individual letters and punctuation would have been impossible without it. With the typewriter, and now the word processor, the poet can fully exploit the spatial possibilities of a blank sheet of white paper; the page itself enters into the composition of

the poem. Since poets began composing on the typewriter, many have used the blank space, the isolated line or word, and the pregnant indentation to poetic and rhythmic advantage.

(Gross and McDowell 1996, 124)

And second, the influence of the French Symbolists (Apollinaire's *Calligrams*, Rimbaud's *Illuminations*, Baudelaire's *Le Spleen de Paris*, et al.), with their eschewing of traditional verse and experiments in typography and/or prose poetry, found its way to British and American Modernist poets such as William Carlos Williams, T. S. Eliot, and Gertrude Stein (*Spring and All*, *The Waste Land*, and *Tender Buttons*, respectively), for whom fragmentation and white space represented a loss of traditional coherence. The combination of these two led to a critical mass of innovative work often included as early examples of flash or lyric nonfiction, and from there, the practice spread.

But while the use of white space has spread, discussion of its craft—the why and how of its use—has lagged behind for writers of prose. Graphic designers and those who do publication layout refer to the white spaces of the page as "functional white." In what ways is it functioning?

In her essay "Is Genre Ever New? Theorizing the Lyric Essay in Its Historical Context," Joanna Eleftheriou finds "As early as 1988, [semiotician R. Lane] Kauffmann argued that essayistic fragmentation has a twofold purpose: it 'preserves freedom of imagination' and 'signals that the knowing subject in the process no longer plays the constitutive role reserved for it in idealist systems, but that it defers instead to the object of cognition'" (Eleftheriou 2016). So, if white space is including the reader in its imagination and deferring meaning-making to them, what is the use of white space requiring of its readers, and what are the effects on them?

Inevitably, the reader will try to assemble a coherent arc or narrative out of the pieces: poet, critic, and MacArthur grantee Heather McHugh (quoted in Burd) says "We can't help, as readers (or as spectators, for that matter—the science of moving pictures was predicated on this fact) putting together the separate frames into a coherent or continuous experience. For the mind is not only analytic but synthetic" (Burd 2015). But does the need to create coherence override the use of white space to create apposition or disrupture? And how can we ensure readers will pay attention, particularly when disrupture, not coherence, is intended? Poet Jane Hirshfield gets at this when she exhorts readers to pay attention to a poem's silences: "This aspect of poetry, too, involves wandering and indirection: to read a poem well, we must travel through its words but also pass through its silences, into the unlocked storehouse of self. Not everything will be given—some part of a poem's good weight will be found outside the poem, in us" (Hirshfield 1997, 114–15). It appears there's a great need to teach readers of creative nonfiction, and especially of lyric essays, how to listen to and read white space, not only words.

This need not be pedantic drudgery. One of the effects of this may be pleasure. In "Crafting Digression: Interactivity and Gamification in Creative Nonfiction," where she treats this text-reader interaction as a form of play, Vivian Wagner explains how,

> In contemporary creative nonfiction, white space is, perhaps, one of the most powerful uses of digressive rhetoric. This might seem counter-intuitive, since white space is *blank*. There seems to be nothing there, digressive or otherwise. In fact, though, white space requires the reader to make connections, guess at meanings, and create a narrative. White spaces allow the reader to make all kinds of conjectures, some of which could exist in the text—whatever that might mean, given the hermeneutics of interpretation—but many of which are, by necessity, created from scratch in the process of reading. And in that interactivity, there's pleasure, and the potential for readerly engagement. As Dinty Moore says in "Positively Negative," an essay on white space, "Readers are smart. They want to participate and want the pleasure of putting two and two together themselves, of making discoveries along the way—sometimes along with the writer and sometimes a step ahead of the writer." In white space, according to Moore, via composition theorist Peter Elbow, there's the "energy of the jump"—the power to be had in making sense of something that is, literally, not there.
>
> (Wagner 2018)

While this passage also assumes a reader will be trying to create a coherent narrative out of a piece using white space—and traditional narrative likely is not the aim in a lyric essay—the point about pleasure is a powerful one, especially if readers are prompted to pay attention to white spaces—to listen to silences, to determine the energy of that jump—as well as to the words.

Another possibility is that white space will create a feeling of unsettledness in the reader because of the meaning-making demands put on them—this may be anxiety on the reader's part, but it may also be an entirely intended effect crafted by the author. Wagner notes how Boully's *The Body: An Essay* does so:

> *The Body* changes the interactivity quotient of nonfiction, since it, with its white space and elisions, requires a great deal of meaning-making from readers. . . . [Boully's text] exists *only* in the footnotes. This technique requires the reader both to imagine the primary text and to live with the unsettledness that comes from knowing there *is* no primary text.
>
> (Wagner 2018)

If the reader can be convinced that the white spaces are crafted as part of the text, and the payoff for engaging with them is equal to or greater than the amount of work or unsettledness the reader puts into it, then the reader will continue to do so. As flash writer Kathy Fish puts it,

> All flash invites collaboration with the reader, but the segmented form especially so. The human brain unconsciously processes about 11 million pieces of information per *second*. So in that tiny pause between fragments a *lot* is happening inside your reader's head. The brain is momentarily freed up to react, insinuate, infer, connect, gather, intuit, deduce, ponder, and, importantly: *feel*.
>
> (Fish 2021)

The problem comes when the reader can determine no clear reason for the white space to exist, an issue poetry form and theory expert Paul Fussell calls out in his foundational 1965 text *Poetic Meter and Poetic Form*:

> [T]he white space. . .means something. If nothing is conceived to be taking place within it, if no kind of silent pressure or advance or reconsideration or illumination or perception seems to be going on

in that white space, the reader has a legitimate question to ask: Why is that white space there, and what am I supposed to do with it?

(Fussell 1965, 155)

In less-experienced hands, white space stands in for a lazy transition the author doesn't know how to make, using the fragmented lyric essay as creative cover for incomplete thought. That, in turn, causes the kind of suspicion of the lyric essay Phillip Lopate expresses (if a bit curmudgeonly): "It seems to me they are angling for a license for their dreamy vagueness, which will allow them to dither on 'lyrically,' trying the patience of most readers. Not that the reader should not be frustrated from time to time, but I prefer that these provocations arise from suspenseful rigor rather than formlessness" (Lopate 2013, 125).

So, outside of lazy transitions, if the white space has an intentional function, what is that function, and how can it be manipulated to create specific effects and engage the reader?

To do this, let's look at some examples and try to break them down. The more I scrutinize examples, it seems like the use of white space operates on a continuum between *content* and *movement*. By content, I mean that the space has its own semiotics—rather than an absence of language, it is a language of absence, by turns representing a whole, specific idea beyond the capability of the words and/or a loss of that wholeness. By movement, I refer to the energy the white space embodies or leverages, which includes (but is not limited to) the transition, digression, turn, shift of expectation, pacing, or leap.

Leaning More Toward Content

First, let's look at the content end of the use of white space continuum. What is contained in such spaces? Because outside of simply lazy transitions, the white space does contain something intentional, whether unsaid or elided, or a pregnant silence.

The Unsaid

Claudia Rankine's *Citizen* is full of such white spaces, but while they allude to a larger context, it's completely clear what's been left unsaid, which is wholly present:

In line at the drugstore it's finally your turn, and then it's not as he walks in front of you and puts his things on the counter. The cashier says, Sir, she was next. When he turns to you he is truly surprised.

Oh my God, I didn't see you.

You must be in a hurry, you offer.

No, no, no, I really didn't see you.

> (Rankine 2014, 77, [text takes up about a third of the page and the rest is blank])

Because the cashier's dialogue is contained within the text of the first paragraph, the spacing of the interaction between the speaker and the other customer appears to be deliberate. As a result, the space enacts his erasure of her. Even as she generously "offers" him an excuse to undo this erasure, he negates the offer ("No, no, no") before reiterating the erasure, followed by a blank rest of the page, the white public space.

I acknowledge the question of white space as a racial issue—words existing against a space of Whiteness, a space dominated by White structures of power and privilege—as foregrounded in Jennifer De Leon's essay collection *White Space: Essays on Race, Culture, and Writing*—and realize this is a larger application which is at play in several of the examples I will be discussing. I will not, however, be focusing on this racial application, as I am neither qualified nor the best theorist for this. However, there is no mistaking what is contained in these spaces and the fact that she doesn't say it, doesn't need to, gives the unsaid more power.

Sun Yung Shin's hybrid memoir *Unbearable Splendor*, about the ruptures enacted by transnational, transracial adoption that continue to resonate, is assembled of fragments and white spaces and erasures representing both rupture as well as the missed, elided, and withheld information regarding her adoption, all of which looms large over this collection. In "Exactly Like You," she writes "Infants make memories, memories not accessible to the older mind, but perhaps to other systems of the body." "We cannot find our original

~~family~~ is unknown to us. No access to stories about our fetal life, or to the body of the mother who was the creator, protector, and nurturer of that our life. We were with ~~her~~ Her until we were about _____." "We were born in or around May of 19__. Unknown are our ~~birth date~~ or our ~~name~~. Slipperiness of a ~~shared~~ time" (Shin 2016, 35–6).

Likewise, in "Orphan: The Plural Form," she notes,

> When you type in the word *adoptee* into the Online Etymology Dictionary search you get this: "No matching terms found." But of course it's from *adoption*, L. *adoptere*, "to choose for oneself." *Adoptee* then implies that one has been chosen for someone else's self.
>
> *Adoptee* is a word that sounds unfinished.
> ....
>
> We think that if we keep trying to get closer and closer to those non-memories that we will go back in time and change the course of events.
>
> But there's nothing but blankness.
>
> (Shin 2016, 52–3)

In Nobel Laureate Louise Glück's essay "Disruption, Hesitation, Silence," from her formative craft collection *Proofs and Theories*, "In most writing, talk is energy and stillness its opposite. When poems are difficult, it is often because their silences are complicated. . . . For me, the answer to such moments is not more language." Here, she argues in favor of the brief lyric, as opposed to the predominant form of poetry of the early 1990s: the long, narrative poem "packed with information" and "exhaustive detail." In contrast, she says, "The unsaid, for me, exerts great power. . . . It is analogous to the unseen; for example, to the power of ruins, to works of art either damaged or incomplete. Such works inevitably allude to larger contexts; they haunt because they are not whole, though wholeness is implied" (Glück 1994, 73, 82). While I agree the unsaid, as a form of white space in nonfiction, alludes to a larger context, I'm not sure I agree with Glück that its use means that a piece is not whole—it does exert power, it does haunt, but only *because* the unsaid has such a specific, intentional presence/meaning, in the way that lace depends on holes as part of its pattern. However, I will be discussing the issue of perceived "wholeness" later in this piece.

The unsaid or elided is eminently present in Boully's *The Body: An Essay*, a book-length lyric essay composed entirely of footnotes. Here, we recall what Wagner said earlier about the "unsettledness" this creates in readers trying to imagine a primary text when "there *is* no primary text." However, I disagree with Wagner about that last part: while readers may not be able to imagine the precise primary text, I would argue what isn't there is made palpable via its referents in the footnotes. Rather than there being "no primary text," I imagine Boully's writing process for this essay being analogous to that of composer John Cage, who claimed that he composed all the notes that comprise *4'33"*—also called the "Silent Sonata"—but that they were all silent. This kind of silence has its own quantitative value and meaning. Poet Jane Hirshfield, too, subscribes to the less-is-more model of the unsaid. In "Poetry and the Mind of Indirection," she asserts, "Poetry, Pound has written, is compression. By how much is left out, we may measure how much is there" (Hirshfield 1997, 114).

Silence

After composing *4'33"*, John Cage gave his "Lecture on Silence," which reiterates this tension of using language, and even punctuation, to create and point to silence—though in this case to appreciate the quality of silence itself:

> What we re-quire   is
> silence;   ;   but what silence requires
>   is   that I go on talking   .
>   (Cage 1959)

In contrast to white space containing a specifically intended but unsaid or elided text, there are white spaces that represent an intent to *not speak*—not to withhold, but to hold space.

Ander Monson does this in his essay "I in River," a piece printed on two-page spreads across the inside margin of the facing pages' shared gutter. You read it by following a chunk of right-justified text on the left page/verso, then crossing over the gutter to read the next chunk or fragment (left-justified on the right page/recto), then back, in a zig-zagging pattern that mimics the meander of a river, though Monson occasionally continues text across both pages in a continuous line. But the layout creates white space between the text fragments on each discrete page and also calls attention to the normally invisible white space of the gutter which operates as the referenced "channel." In doing so, Monson makes the white space palpable, in order to expound on the role of water in the desert: "The Rillito River does not channel water through semiarid Tucson much of the year. It once did. . . . But the channel's there, isn't it. . . ." "It's fair to say I didn't think much about water before moving to Arizona, where water means absence, means scarcity, means conservation, except when it monsoons, and the river runs high." "So which is the river, we ask: the channel or the water?" In fact, he makes explicit his use of white space, making visible its transparency, to highlight how he's making this palpable (I've used slashmarks to indicate where text jumps across the gutter): "a pagebreak [pagebreak occurs here] is a designed absence, as is the gutter space. . . . We like containment. We like order. Without order / (form) / there is no shape, no meaning, nothing to resist or push against / or pull across an emptiness. The whitespace makes the text // an island." "It's hard not to be aware / of the absence once you see its extent" (Monson 2020, 25–37).

Terry Tempest Williams, in *When Women Were Birds*, recounts how her dying mother left all her journals to be read only after the coming death. When Williams opens them, she finds all the journals are blank. This revelation stuns her so much she avoids the journals for twenty-five years. Her book, subtitled "Fifty-Four Variations on Voice," is how a daughter who is a writer reckons with that deliberate white space, with her mother's intent to not speak, the silence her choice of voice: "I was aware of the silences within my mother. They were her places of strength, inviolable. . . . When silence is a choice, it is an unnerving presence" (Williams 2012, 16, 24).

Mary Ruefle, in her essay "*My* Emily Dickinson," describes this tension in terms of both space and sound: "this *literacy of death* is self-consciousness in dialogue with its opposite, the absence of consciousness. [This dialogue is] one in which the writer begins by *speaking* and more and more awakens to *listening*" (Ruefle 2012, 170, italics hers). As the writer learns to listen, so must the reader.

As poet Li-Young Lee explains in "The Pregnant Silence that Opens,"

> I think I'm trying to use words to inflect the silence so that the silence becomes more palpable. I don't think silence is just a lack of sound. . . . It's like when sculptors use rock—stone—in order for us to experience space. You know the Gothic cathedrals? When you walk into them, it's space you experience. The verticality of space, but they achieve it by using rock. Otherwise you can't point to it. It's transparent. Art uncovers space, silence. We're using words to make the silence palpable.
>
> (Lee 2006, 122)

Doing Both Content and Movement

In the middle of the continuum, white space functions both as content (as described above) as well as to create movement. To return to Jorie Graham's "Some Notes on Silence," she asserts, "I need to feel the places where the language fails, as much as one can. Silence which is awe or astonishment, the speech ripped out of you. . . . Its emissaries are the white space, of course, the full stops. . . . I'd like to think you can feel, by its accurate failures, the forces pressing against the sentence, the time order" (Graham 1984, 409). That phrase "accurate failures," points to white space as a conscious craft choice made in order to represent that failure and put pressure on the language around it.

In Theresa Cha's *Dictee*, the title itself speaks to the difficulty or failure of language: it means "dictation" in French, but in a book-length hybrid work that includes English, Korean, Chinese, and French and covers the imperialisms of China, Japan, America, and the Catholic Church, the title implies this language is imposed by dictate. Jennifer Lee Tsai points out how the epilogue section "Diseuse" captures the difficulty of the immigrant speech act: when Cha writes "Open paragraph It was the first day period She had come from a far period " (Cha 2001, 1), Tsai notes how "this compels the reader to consider the arbitrary, ideologically enforced conventions that often govern language and writing. Additionally, this opening passage illustrates the difficulty of communication and expression for the 'She' who 'had come from a far', the nameless immigrant figure who is linguistically and politically disenfranchised and displaced." In describing the rest of *Dictee*, Tsai says that it points to inherent limitations in representing the postcolonial, diasporic subject. Additionally, this illustrates the problematic nature inherent in the act of speaking on behalf of silenced Korean women which exposes power relations between Cha as author/critic and the historical displacement of Korean women. These are acknowledged in the visual representation of gaps and silences by use of white space in between words, sentences and pages (Tsai 2023). Eula Biss's fragmentary essay "Time and Distance Overcome" juxtaposes scenes of telephone poles linked to violence to complicate the ideas of connection and division at the birth of telephony, the resistance to forward movement mimicking resistance to (and, in the case of racism, a lack of) progress (Biss 2008). The fragments themselves function like telephone poles, stringing their connections across the dividing white space—what is communicated? Or is failed to communicate?

As Jennifer Burd puts it, in her essay "White Space as Metaphorical Frame," "White space is where the words it frames resonate with contextual, associational, and emotional meaning" (Burd 2015). In terms of the continuum of white space usage, those resonances are contained within the white space itself (violence, disconnect, failure of progress of communication) as well as in the energy movement from one fragment to the next, depending on whether the contextual or associational meanings are shifting between juxtaposed texts (bridge, shift, leap).

This tension between white space and the words it frames, or the words framed by it, is most tightly strung in Anne Carson's monument to absence, her book-arts artifact *Nox*: a collage of classical and personal history and ephemera that visually represents with omnipresent white spaces the estranged silences, inexplicable absences, and sudden death of her brother (Carson 2010).

Movement

Again, Jennifer Burd: "We feel how a word framed by white space resonates against the words coming before and after it, *across* the distance of the white space" (Burd 2015). But what kind of energy resonates across these white spaces? Or, in another sense, what kind of movement occurs? Some ways we might describe the energy or movement the white space embodies or leverages includes (but is not limited to) the transition, bridge, digression, turn, shift of expectation, pacing, or leap. But in order to determine the type of movement, it's left to the reader to determine whether the fragments are being placed in juxtaposition, apposition, opposition, sequence, or something else.

To return to Robert Root from the beginning, he defines segmented essays as "sometimes called collage essays or disjunctive essays or paratactic essays" and thinks of white space as the silence or physical space that separates them into discrete segments like the movements of a concerto or panels of a medieval triptych, with the space as "rests," "gaps," and "uncertainty." But the energies named as "collage," "disjunctive," or "paratactic" are quite different: juxtaposition, opposition, and apposition, respectively. The spaces between these would resonate differently between each of these. Imagine it as the space between magnets: juxtaposition would be neutral, while opposition would be a repelling energy, and apposition would be attractive.

For example, in Claudia Rankine's *Citizen*, the white spaces between the sections and fragments act like apposition: not a sequence, but an accretion of experiences of racial aggressions both micro and macro, a wearying and horrific *and and and*. In contrast, Sun Yung Shin's use of white space often feels like oppositional energy, the fragments resisting each other just as her search for identity and culture is a constant encounter with resistance. Here, I think especially of Kathy Fish's flash piece "Collective Nouns for Humans in the Wild" and its startling catalogue of proposed names for groups shifting subtly between fragments, from whimsical to more serious, before culminating in a gutpunch of a shift at the end. In fact, in this example, it's the white space that creates the gutpunch, with its pacing, pause, and then succinct, deadly delivery. The final line should by every logic be oppositional, but because of the building appositions of the three previous "targets," the final one becomes the sickening outcome of the sequence (Fish 2017).

Of Fragments and Segments

Essays using a lot of white space are often described as fragmented, or as Amy Bonnaffons says, "The result of breakage: a proliferation of edge, of space" (Bonnaffons 2016). But Robert Root uses the term "segmented essay" or "segment," as opposed to "fragment," in his "This Is What the Spaces Say," and Randon Billings Noble categorizes such pieces as "Segmented" in her anthology *A Harp in the Stars: An Anthology of Lyric Essays*, though she notes, as does Root, that such essays are also called fragmented, paratactic, or collage (Noble 2021, xiv–xv). This seeming conflation of terms returned to me during a Q&A after a multi-author reading that included Elissa Washuta. I asked a question about the authors' use of fragmentation, and how they saw fragments functioning in their writing. Washuta responded that she doesn't think of her work as fragmentation but as segments with leaps between them. She added that she thinks of segments as longer, a page or more (Washuta 2021). Her distinction got me wondering about the difference, if any, between segments and fragments. Is there a difference in the quality or quantity of white space in a piece, and what it indicates about the text?

Segment comes from the Latin *secare*, "to cut," while fragment is from *frangere*, "to break." Both suggest separate pieces. But what is the role of agency in each? Is there more of a surgical intent in cutting your writing into segments? Is breaking more violent—to be ripped, shattered—what Sam Cha, in his fragmented essay on Shin's fragmented collection, calls "Torn into sections. . . . A torn form for the torn identity" (Cha 2019)? And who does the breaking—the author? Or is the content already broken, and the brokenness is what's being represented—Sam Cha's "an immigrant mode, an exile's mode" (Cha 2019)? It is our attempts to answer these questions—about the way they're separated, and how we characterize the energy of that separation—that get at how white space is operating here.

Joanna Eleftheriou demonstrates how the need for naming the "lyric essay," despite leading to its branding under D'Agata, made it possible to theorize about the lyric essay and its features. In it, she says "we theorize how a fragmented structure permits representation of selves that claim to be experienced as fragmentary, or as having restricted access to their own (frequently traumatic) memories. . . . Remaining faithful to the impossibility of representation permits the lyric essay, also, to convey the experience of the victim, whose violation often causes a rupture between self and world" (Eleftheriou 2016). Sandra Beasley posits a similar use: "On a pragmatic level, here are some circumstances in which the lyric essay might prove advantageous: The essay concerns a personal episode in which the author lacked power. Lyric moves, particularly fragmentation and passive voice, enact a lack of agency on the page" (Beasley 2014).

This raises the question: Are fragments necessarily informed by trauma? And if so, what is the relationship of the white space between fragments to fractures, ruptures, fault lines, sutures? Are they characterized by violence, despite an attempt to heal that breakage—call it a suture, a scar?

And what then of Elissa Washuta's work? By cutting her traumatic experiences into what she distinguishes as segments, is Washuta exerting more control or agency over her material? By this logic, am I saying Shin, Monson, and Biss exert less control? Because that doesn't seem right. Perhaps they're making the breakage more visible? This also suggests that the less text, and the more fragmented a text is, and the more white space there is as a result, the more charged that space is.

Issue of Wholeness versus Loss of Wholeness

Perhaps the problem of the ratio of white space to text stems from an issue of perceived wholeness: whether a text in segments or fragments represents a whole experience, or a loss of wholeness, and whether one suggests more "wholeness" than the other. Eleftheriou concurs: "Reckoning with fragments (and the elusive illusion of wholeness) is something the lyric essay can do, and its connection to the history of the fragment both before and after the Romantic era merits further attention" (Eleftheriou 2016). Montaigne's fragments, written to represent the inevitable decay of memory and time, suggest that he saw the form as representing a lack of wholeness.

By the Romantics, the pendulum has swung the other way: Schlegel's embrace and imitation of the surviving fragments of classical literary texts (like those of Sappho) suggest a sort of sublime chaos that contains and represents a dialectic with a whole beyond the fragments (cf. Eleftheriou 2016). Then back again: the Modernist fragment is about *loss* of wholeness, the artist a *bricoleur* assembling the broken world of the Industrial Revolution and World War I into something else: Eliot's "these fragments I have shored against my ruin." Language poet and theorist Ann Lauterbach, in a Q&A, said,

> in the Modernist idea the fragment was really about the lament for the lost whole narrative, the historical narrative. So at the very end of *The Cantos* when Pound says, "I cannot make it cohere," it's a crucial moment for him because it's a moment where he understands a new nature of the fragment. A fragment is a discrete whole, a gesture that offers vitality and variety, multiple perspectives and disparate vocabularies not bound to predicates of sense.
> (Lauterbach 1999b)

In this sense, there *isn't* a connection across white space between fragments—each fragment is "a discrete whole" in itself, but it does not "cohere" to the others to make a larger whole, a narrative.

Finally, the contemporary impulse seems to be a return to wholeness, or at least a wholeness that honors the breakage as part of the intentional design, a sort of *kintsugi*, what Heather McHugh calls "a declared partiality." In the introduction to her *Broken English: Poetry and Partiality*, she asserts,

> [Poetry] is a broken language from the beginning, brimming with non-words: all that white welled up to keep the line from surrendering to the margin; all that quiet, to keep the musics marked. . . . [Speaking of Dickinson and Celan:] Their lyricisms

are fuller for the spaces, their structure a math of the missing. . . .
It is the space that defines the words, the skull the kiss, the hole
the eye. [S]ilence deepens around Celan's language until we feel
life itself is only briefly spared. Dickinson's characteristically
terse structures. . .generate so many mutually resistant and yet
simultaneous readings.

(McHugh 1993, viii–ix)

Ann Lauterbach goes further: "For a while I have been interested in the notion of a whole fragment." In "On Flaws: Toward a Poetics of the Whole Fragment," an essay presented in fragments (as indicated by slashmarks here), she starts by describing purchasing an item marked "as is": "'As is' indicates that / the object. . .has a flaw. . . / As is suggests the distance from perfection from which the object has traveled / through the course of time, its fall from Platonic grace or virgin purity. . . . The lost/found place of 'as is' thus could be seen as a poetic methodology, through which we / might revise the modernist 'fragment'" (Lauterbach 1999a). She clarifies in the Q&A follow up:

> The narrative as story had been ruptured once and for all; I wanted the gaps to show. When the gaps began to show, a new sense of possibility came forward in which mobile units were suspended in time and space. In the new syntactical dispensation, hinges or places of contact became an important location of meaning, as in musical composition. . . . I began to perceive that the fragments among which we live are cause for celebration rather than lament.
>
> (Lauterbach 1999b)

This idea of "whole fragment" may provide a third and neutral option: more recently, critics and writers have theorized a rhizomatic model, based on fungal networks. As Amy Bonnaffons suggests, "we might view the recent emergence of networks and rhizomes as evidence that there are more ways of conceiving of structures— more ways of reading—than we might have previously granted" (Bonnaffons 2016). In this case, the fragments would represent the mushrooms, the fruiting bodies popping up, seemingly random yet connected and communicating below the surface, invisible in the white space. This assumes neither a positive value nor negative value—the fragments may still be based in decay, a form of Joyelle McSweeney's "necropastoral"—but simply another way to conceptualize the fragmented essay: not a whole that has been broken, but as content that is an organic whole, connected in the writer's mind, but of which we are only seeing what text the writer chooses to reveal.

So, it does appear that the more white space—the less "whole" the text appears, the more fragmented, the more visible the breakage—the more charged that space becomes. However, that also means more work on the part of the reader, who must determine how the pieces (segments, fragments) relate—and with fragments, there often is less information to go on—and therefore what kind of resonant energy is contained between them, and/or what kind of movement is occurring.

In conclusion, while I've tried to amass in this book the discussions taking place, creative nonfiction is still fairly theory-less, still in its early stages. In the case of white space, it's been borrowing heavily from poetry theory. This practice may be without consciously realizing it, as poets move to writing lyric nonfiction with these craft usages internalized, or it may simply be unacknowledged, as in the cases of Root and D'Agata. If we can identify and study these craft elements—both as they're used in poetry, and how they're being imported and used in creative nonfiction—we can better understand how to apply these strategies, and how to read them when we encounter them. Specifically, we need to make writers and readers of creative nonfiction and especially the lyric essay aware of the continuum in use of white space—the difference between the unsaid and silence, the different flavors of silence, and the different energies of motion across white spaces—so that both writers are more thoughtful in how and why they're employing it and readers know what they're reading and listening for and can trust the writer's intent, rather than concluding "there is no there there."

Fragmentation Grenade: The Violence of Hybridity

On Uses of Space: *Lyric*

with thanks to Nomi Stone

Nomi and I come together on hybridity—a form, a site, where disparate elements come together.

She says hybridity is treated as freedom, but often, what goes unacknowledged is its violence. These two concepts also come together in the hybrid. They collude. They collide.

Hybridity as collision, infarction, infection.

Nomi and I are considering my "Consider the Lobster Mushroom," a hybrid piece about hybrids using the metaphor of the lobster mushroom which, "contrary to its common name, is not a mushroom but the result of a parasitic fungus having infested a host mushroom in a peculiar symbiosis." It ends, "Is this a craft essay infected by a lyric essay, or a lyric essay infected by a craft essay?"

Joyelle McSweeney's necropastoral, the *cordon sanitaire* revealed as permeable membrane easily pierced, infiltrated, infected (McSweeney 2014).

Hybridity as moving between forms, unfreely. Transformation as a kind of violence. Andersen's mermaid de-tailed, each human step like stepping on swords. Ovid's *Metamorphoses* as origin story: Syrinx turned reed, cut and punctured into panpipes; Daphne's skin encrusted with bark. The persistence of psychic experience, how we internalize it; infected by it, it invades our dream spaces.

In *Dictee*, Therese Cha's Korean mother becomes Manchurian; Victoria Chang's parents flee China for the American Dream in *Dear Memory*. Attempts to address and make sense of their memories, a hyperdocumentation of records and stories and images, nonetheless can only document what can't be said, a trauma recorded deep in their tree rings.

Nomi and I cross messages on grafting. When grafting trees, the upper part or scion (selected for its superior flowers or fruit) is notched and inserted into the bottom or inferior part or rootstock, a process called inosculation. It sounds pretty, like kissing. But scions are always trying to force kisses onto their inferiors. Ask Daphne about this. Ask Sally Hemings.

The violence of trying to fit content to a certain aesthetic form. The poetics of impurity.

Wendy Rawlings's "Let's Talk About Shredded Romaine Lettuce" tries to twine the narrative of her niece nearly dying of an *E. coli* infection together with iPads and bagged salad, an uneasy alliance that mimics the imbalance between Western consumption and workers' rights. Every time she thinks she has a handle on the topic, another pops up to take its place. At several points she stops, switches tracks, doubles back, then admits "I think I'm losing control of this story."

(Rawlings 2014)

Hydra, she of branched heads ever-sprouting who cannot be controlled, daughter of the half-snake half-woman-bodied Echidna, mother of monstrous births.

The French bulldog, most popular dog in America, is bred for a certain aesthetic form—small, stocky, with broad square-shaped heads and short noses—despite how the puppies' broad, square-shaped heads can't be birthed, must be cut from their mothers' small, stocky bodies to fulfill Western consumption.

Sometimes unstable content can only give birth to itself, breaking or tearing through form in a way that leaves a trace, a wave of mutilation.

Both West and East have engaged in rape as a weapon of war, during invasions and colonizations.

Both West and East currently engage in hybrid warfare, hydra-headed: a blend of unconventional destabilizing techniques—propaganda, deception, cyberattacks, sabotage—as well as conventional weapons. Hail Hydra. The failure of authoritarianism pitting against the failure of democracy. Both election hacking and fragmentation grenades leave ragged edges.

I think I'm losing control of this essay.

Hybridity as painful failure to contain, documenting its own failure. The fragmented language betrayals of Lee Ann Roripaugh's *Dandarians*. The attempts to negotiate identity as a transnational, transracial adoptee—a birthed body crossing borders—in the fragmented narrative of Sun Yung Shin's *Unbearable Splendor*. Boully's *The Body*, accessible only via the fragments of footnotes. A rearticulation. Recently, Boully tweeted:

> When I was sending out excerpts of The Body, one editor, who is a famous writer, wrote on the rejection slip, "I don't even know what this is."
>
> I saved that rejection like a love letter.
> (@JennyBoully, February 3, 2022)

Fragment, from *frangere*, "to break." Is breaking more violent—to be ripped, shattered—what Sam Cha, in his fragmented essay on Sun Yung Shin's collection, calls "Torn into sections.... A torn form for the torn identity" (Cha 2019)? While hybridity might be freeing for some, a gentle blend or blur of boundaries, the form which is not one, it also may be the best form to represent rupture. It's the fragments that do the most damage, splintering, ripping through the body of a piece.

Is this a craft essay infected by a lyric essay? Or a violent joining, signifying scar?

A Dash of Dash: The Lyric Art of Punctuation

with apologies to Noah Lukeman

Before evolving to mark syntax for you, silent reader—hearing these lines in your head, perhaps in a version of your own voice, or perhaps one you've invented to suit me (how do I sound to you?)—punctuation began as a guide to reading aloud, akin to musical notation, indicating breath breaks and rhetorical shifts, differences in pitch: verbal stage directions. Punctuation as punctum, existing all at one point, until ... expanding infinitely outward across the emptiness of the page's space, inflecting it with flavors of pause and visibility.

(Lyric, not Lukeman's *Style*, whose focus is prose.)

- The period. Hard transition. Hard pause. Hard pacing. Punctuation's menarche and yet a hard stop.

    Shorter, more frequent periods. A sign of immaturity. This age's short attention span. Whereas sentences with more to say, more content, more content to extend, and therefore with less periods, seem either sophisticated or a sign of a bygone style.

    Ironically, cf. heavy periods. Cf. a more muscular, masculine style. Cf. Hemingway, Carver.

    The period is a boundary. Diana is the goddess of boundaries, including menarche and menopause. The start and end of periods. The boundary's boundaries.

:
;
Still other softer stops, stacked vertically: the divisive colon and semicolon, who divide readers and even writers; yet they point to something on the other side of the divide, try to hold hands with it through the tiny gap. Lukeman describes the semicolon as elegant, aesthetically pleasing, a luxury item, and says its primary function is to connect; he then criticizes those who overuse it, especially writers of the early twentieth century. Yet for them, there was no other way; only connect. The semicolon enables more complex thought; it invites the reader into the intimate inner sanctum of the writer's unspooling mind. Yet the colon is the elegant semicolon's wild younger sister: all melodrama, making a scene or making a statement on the way out: a gasped intake before the big reveal. The diva delivers her great aria and then: the curtain call.

Multiple colons in lyric writing create: a string of thoughts: a throughline: a thread to be threaded through those dots.

,
The comma, little breath mark, noted between notes, in pencil, on my flute music, quick gasp, impeding the flow. A pause, as of musical phrasing, or a signature, of time, passing. If music is audible math, the comma both adds, as well as divides, the enumerated.

Lukeman says, "The writer who overuses commas tends to also overuse adjectives and adverbs. . . . He grasps for multiple word choices" (Lukeman 2006, 65). While I feel called out, despite not being the He of all Lukeman's conjectured writers, I also feel it important to note, that the comma is crucial to lateral movement, essential to slippage, to the sideways sidle, the appositive accrual, for which multiple word choices (and genders) are critical.

( )   Parentheses, a containment field (who or what is being contained?), a flex (the material so strong it presses outward), a tender aside (only you and I are invited within its intimate bounds). (Is what's inside more, or less, important?)

Lukeman sees parentheses and double dashes as nearly identical in effect—"virtually interchangeable" (114)—but does he see them? What about the visual? A selfie in a convex mirror.

( ) shaped like ears to be whispered into, a spoken-but-overheard quality, an aside, a digression.

Lukeman says the writer who overuses parentheses thinks in digression, "overflowing with knowledge, impatient to get it all in." (As if that's a bad thing.) Fragments, half-ideas, running off mid-thought to chase an idea down the rabbit hole (and somewhere, down there (the wild hair (hare (nested)))).

?   Question mark, the riddler of endings, yet perhaps meant as play, as game? A gamine voice lilting upward? If rhetorical, does it not, for moment, create a space inside its hook? A crooked finger inviting you, reader, even briefly, to imagine your answer?

. . .   One period is a hard stop yet ironically not three. . .no neat start but spotting. . .no hard stop at the trailing off of menopause, an ellipses whose spotting points at a stuttering. . . or else three at a time. . .an imbalance that accompanies immaturity, or the overly sentimental.

—   Em-dash—the "Em" short for Emily—who dashed off her hand-sewn fascicles—full of them—little pauses—little stitches in time—making space visible—tension rods in tensile ambivalence—to connect or hold separate?—from "ambi" + "valent" to hold both—committed to refusing to commit—the dash more casual—even dashing—dashing off a point before dashing off—

White space   Zero   at the Bone

/   Like white space a ceasing of sound / a caesura / but more vivid / even violent / call it a *slash* / a collapse of lines pancaked into prose / the layers still visible / literary strata.

*
•   Idiosyncratic dingbats, a doofy name for a discreet divider, dividing text into discrete sections, longer than
❖   a medium pause, may contain a shift of perspective, of style, of time or topic, framing the text in its own cel signaled by this cartoonishly-named device, bullet-riddled stop sign at the edge of town.

Permissive Sieves

Like many writers, I come to the lyric essay from a background as a practicing poet. And the poetry I'm known for practicing often is written in received forms, like the sonnet or triolet, and as such, I'm often tapped to teach poetic forms to students. Last semester, while trying to stretch my teaching and my own writing by teaching a hybrid forms workshop that included the lyric essay, my experience with forms led to two things striking me.

There's an oft-repeated saw (at least by me, to my students, ad nauseum) that originates in a letter from Theodore Roethke: "'Form' is regarded not as a neat mould to be filled, but rather as a sieve to catch certain kinds of material" (Kinzie 1993, 306). Sonnet-sieves catch short arguments or questions to be resolved. Villanelles and triolets strain out all but the most obsessive turnings-over of topics.

Since this is the mindset with which I come to writing, as I was teaching my class, I found myself thinking of the lyric essay as its own poetic form—asking not how to define it as a "mould," but trying to determine what kind of material is suited to its sieve.

To do so, it might help to review the qualities and structural features of the lyric essay, in order to think about what kinds of content they might facilitate. The lyric essay represents a collision of opposites: poetry with prose, music and meaning, the realistic with the speculative. It often presents its material content through parataxis, juxtaposition, fragmentation, and collage in a way that makes representation a dynamic process. Its disjunctive leaps, hesitations, ellipses, elisions, non-sequiturs, and self-contradictions subvert the privileging of writing as the product of the Romantic unified "I." It suppresses linear progression and narrative in favor of circularity, meditation, experience, and imagination.

Yet the lyric essay balances this instability by keeping the reader's attention at the level of language with lexical and syntactical richness, repetitions of sounds, words, phrases, motifs, and braids. What's important emerges through accretion of patterns, either by imposing a pattern on what otherwise appears to be chaos, or by revealing an underlying or hidden pattern. The deceptively simple packaging of prose may use brevity, the speed of its progression, and often colloquial language to persuade the reader to quickly accept any odd or surreal details and/or to move across juxtapositions assuming connections, yet can make surprising turns even more surprising.

As a result of these qualitative and structural features, the lyric essay "sieve" seems to attract or catch the following kinds of material (drawing from Lindner 2012, Lopate 2013, and Sajé 2012):

- The surreal or absurd, either because the subject matter is surreal or absurd or in order to subvert logic or a prevailing paradigm. The speed of the prose moves the reader through its odd logic, while the lyric patterning reveals a larger truth or beauty.

- Embodied oppositions or tensions, within a form that does the same through shifts of point of view, style, tone, and/or collage.

- Meditations, especially where the author isn't sure what they think. The lyric essay allows the author to approach the material from several angles simultaneously (often through lists, fragments, or braids), while the "lyric" poetics attempt to impose or reveal patterns.

The second thing that struck me was the lyric essay's similarity to another poetic form that emerged in American poetry around the same time. The lyric essay was first named by Deborah Tall, then-editor of *Seneca Review*, in 1994, in a note to John D'Agata, and the journal devoted at least part of its space to the hybrid starting in 1997 (Eleftheriou 2016). In 1992 Kashmiri poet Agha Shahid Ali introduced contemporary poets to the medieval Persian form, the ghazal, in an essay "Ghazal: The Charms of a Considered Disunity" (Ali 1992), began publishing his own, and prodded his colleagues to write poems in the form, which he published in the 2000 anthology *Ravishing DisUnities: Real Ghazals in English*.

For those unfamiliar with the ghazal: it is a form written in couplet stanzas, of at least five couplets but with no maximum limit. In the opening couplet, both lines end with a short refrain immediately preceded by a rhyme; in subsequent couplets, only the second line has the rhyme and refrain, and the final couplet often is signaled by incorporating the poet's name. (For several examples, search "ghazal" at the Poetry Foundation's website at poetryfoundation.org.) Yet a hallmark of the form is its seeming *disunity*: as Ali explains, "The ghazal is made up of thematically independent couplets held (as well as not held) together in a stunning fashion.... Then what saves the ghazal from what might be considered arbitrariness? A technical context, a formal unity based on rhyme and refrain and prosody" (Ali 2002, 210).

In both the ghazal and the lyric essay, what's important is what's emphasized by pattern, yet each gives the writer as much or as little room as desired to approach the topic from any number of angles. The effect may be a cohesive progression building on the central theme or refrain idea, or disjunctive fragments linked only by the theme/refrain's central hub. Both invite the reader to engage with the shape, co-creating meaning in determining how the piece hangs, or doesn't hang, together.

In some examples of the lyric essay, the fragments on the page visually resemble the ghazal's brief couplets, as in Fanny Howe's "Doubt" or this excerpt from Claudia Cortese's "The Red Essay":

1) Setting: The barn. Sometimes, I can't remember if there were stars, fall air clear or smoky, the shape of the moon's face.

2) I read Perrault's moral to my students: *Attractive, well-bred young ladies should never talk to strangers, for if they should, they may well provide dinner for the wolf.*

4) Afterward, Bill died, and I was glad. Afterward, he sang Meat Loaf to me and I held him and laughed.

1.5) Other times, I can see the barn door wide open, grass below soaked in starlight. I could have

screamed or clawed. I dreamt saltwater
taffy, sister's sticky kiss, how we kicked
pigeons with our skirts over our heads.

I worried about his feelings, that he'd feel rejected.

3) I said, *Let's go back to the house. I'm cold. Please. Stop.* He said, *It won't take long. I won't go in all the way.* We negotiated. What do you name that?

(Cortese 2013, 25–6)

In this excerpt, Cortese holds in tension trauma memoir and fairytale, anecdote and critique, prose and poetic fragments, linked by the motifs of the wolf and vulnerable girl, and by the proper nouns she does name—Perrault, Bill, Meat Loaf—even as she struggles to name her experience. Other lyric essays don't use fragments but incorporate thematically or stylistically autonomous parts to achieve tension. Each section of Nicole Walker's brief triptych "Fish" approaches its common subject from a different point of view and a nonfiction style—nature documentary, memoir, food writing—but ties the three sections together through motifs and words that echo throughout the piece: the act of straining, "flesh," "hold," "circling" (Walker 2013). Likewise, Brian Doyle's moving 9/11 essay "Leap" links a collage of eyewitness accounts, apocalyptic biblical quotes, and meditative speculation via the repetition of "hand in hand" to transform the horror of bodies leaping from the Twin Towers into a prayerful, elegiac image (Doyle 2003, 129–31).

The above examples lend themselves to what Wordsworth critic Wimsatt called "process of mind": they demonstrate the experience of a mind exploring and discovering a complex topic, and they engage the reader in this process. That both the lyric essay and the ghazal reached a critical mass in popularity at the same moment may signal a readiness for forms which, as Agha Shahid Ali puts it, "evade the Western penchant for unity" (211), whether unity of speaker, style, or source—forms which allow for a multifaceted exploration of its content. To return to Ali, as he phrases the question, "Do such freedoms frighten some of us?" (212).

Strike a Chord: The Lyre That Makes the Lyric

On Resonance: Traditional

The lyric essay is usually considered alongside the prose poem and the flash essay, among other hybrids, occupying that gray space on the continuum between poetry and prose. Often it is characterized by its brevity, though book-length lyric essays exist (Maggie Nelson's *Bluets*, N. Scott Momaday's *The Way to Rainy Mountain*, Anne Carson's *Nox*), so length can't be the main distinction. It also experiences overlap with the prose poem, though the latter may or may not deal with nonfictional matter—the lyric essay is an *essay*, not just prose. Yet it's not the same thing as flash nonfiction either, despite all these terms getting used interchangeably. So where length and subject matter cannot be determinants, rather than the *essay* we must look at the *lyric* part, an element under-examined and -theorized even as it has been attached to *essay* with abandon. This may be because prose writers also deal in images and symbols, so they're not totally foreign—the lyric essay merely implies a greater density of these. But what of sound? As Judith Kitchen noted,

> The term [lyric essay] had been minted (brilliantly, it seems to me) by Deborah Tall, then almost immediately undermined. Not all essays are lyric. Repeat. Not all essays are lyric. Not even all short essays are lyric. Some are merely short. Or plainly truncated. Or purely meditative. Or simply speculative. Or. Or. Or. But not lyric. Because, to be lyric, there must be a lyre.
>
> (Kitchen 2007, 47)

While some of the terms that describe sonic resonance are recognizable, in a lit class vocabulary kind of way (rhyme, refrain, alliteration), they reside in the realm of poetics. In fact, *The New Princeton Encyclopedia of Poetry and Poetics* puts it rather passionately, for a reference book: "The words in poetry are words not because they express meaning—they do that in prose—but because they are also sound, because they take their life in sound. It is as sound that they teach us what words are" (Preminger and Brogan 1993, 1179). What I aim to do here is to import poetry craft's definitions of these musical elements to show how images and motifs mimic this sonic patterning, and how the use of both adds resonance, to create the *lyric* part of the lyric essay.

A lot of what's useful in understanding the lyric essay comes from poetics discussions of the lyric as a mode, as well as of free verse and prose poetry, where critics have examined how, in the absence of meter and traditional received forms, poets fall back on other forms of patterning to create and sustain lyric movement and tension.

Lyric, as a mode, depends on resonance of sound and image, the symbol of the lyre strings, strummed. Poet Katharine Coles, in her craft essay "If a Body," asserts "'lyric' as a noun . . . for me . . . indicates a reliance on dense musicality and imagery" (Coles 2019). Diana Wilson, in "Laces in the Corset," a discussion of the "Structures of Poetry and Prose that Bind the Lyric Essay," describes most of her examples she studies in terms of synonyms for resonance—repetition, recurring, reflexive, connective, retrospective-prospective—though she tends to focus on visual resonances of images, rather than sonic resonance (Wilson 2015). I want to combine both: I find Coles's argument compelling, and I like the terminology employed by Wilson though I want to expand it to include the musical, the sonic. Together, they create an argument for *lyric* comprising densely repeating patterns. Resonance.

It's not enough that the lyric essay merely include these resonant elements—they must repeat enough to create sonic and/or semantic patterns. One of the most prolific poet-critics of the late twentieth century, John Hollander, in his important text *Melodious Guile*, contends "that the energies of patterning are necessary to poetic representations is undeniable." In the chapter "Garlands of Her Own," he gets at how seemingly "free" literary forms nonetheless impose their own patterns:

> Free verse, according to Robert Frost, is like playing tennis without a net, but that is true only of bad writing of any kind. Good free verse is like playing a new game, without a net but with an intricately mapped court, far more complex than that ruled by the lines of a tennis court, and a strict set of rules of another sort.
>
> (Hollander 1988, 90)

Equally important critic Paul Fussell, in the indispensable *Poetic Meter and Poetic Form*, pushes in further: "free verse lines, deprived of pattern in one dimension, the metrical, tend to compensate by employing another kind of pattern, conspicuous repetition of phrases or syntactical forms. A special kind of significant repetition is almost the hallmark of a certain school of modern free verse" (Fussell 1965, 79).

But any pattern, adhered to too strictly, becomes lulling, even numbing, which is why writers using them often employ a theme-and-variations approach, and/or disrupt their patterns in strategic ways. As poet and essayist Camille T. Dungy explains in her craft essay "Tell It Slant,"

> The beauty of repetition lies in the occasional disruption of repetition: Expectation and reward. Expectation and reward. Expectation, expectation. Surprise! A writer might build a little nest in a poem, a comfortable place for the reader's mind to rest (the material for this nest might be rhyme, might be repetition of words or phrases, might be consistency of images or ideas), but . . . too much comfort breeds disinterest.
>
> Create a pattern, reward that pattern, and disrupt that pattern—but rather than leaving the poem in that state of disruption, return to the pattern.
>
> (Dungy 2014)

In the absence of overt poetic structures—lines/line breaks (though there may be fragments), stanzas, meter, received forms—the lyric essay must turn, and return, to these patterns for its lyric impact. And they must return within close enough proximity for the reader's eye/ear/mind to pick up on it.

To the pattern elements Dungy lists above—refrains and the rhyming of words or images or ideas—I would add anaphora (specifically, repetition of the initial word or phrase of a sentence or fragment), alliteration/assonance/consonance, wordplay of homophones (including their connotation/denotation), and cadence/rhythm. I'm going to review these various types of resonance, with explanations and brief examples, before I take a closer look at a few key lyric essay passages to help illustrate how I see these elements functioning in the lyric essay. (Note: Scaffolding lyric essays on certain poetic forms, or using the sonic effects of white space and/or punctuation, also add to the lyric resonance of an essay. But since I cover these topics in other essays, I will not be discussing them here.) Applying these patterning elements to create resonance in readings is key, because "pattern organizes, highlights, and intensifies meaning in all verbal strings. This suggests that it is necessary, even essential, to study pattern, and dangerous to study it in isolation from meaning for very long" (Preminger and Brogan 1993, 1176).

Refrain

A refrain is a word or phrase repeated either verbatim or with slight variations—in poetry, refrains often occur at regular intervals (Preminger and Brogan 1993, 1018). Hollander's chapter "Breaking into Song: Some Notes on Refrain" does an excellent job of explaining how refrain functions in a poem. In speaking about Poe and the refrain "Nevermore" in "The Raven," he describes how even a verbatim refrain can develop over the course of a piece: "Poe went on to observe of his broken refrain that its 'application'—as he called its syntactic, logical, and rhetorical role *in situ* of each strophe that it concluded—was to vary, even as the word itself remained unchanged" (Hollander 1988, 131).

In order to frame the question that must be asked of all refrains, Hollander draws a key distinction: as opposed to meaningless refrains that merely hold space (like "fa-la-la"), "Poetic refrain, on the other hand, starts out by troping the literalness of the repetition, by raising a central parabolic question for all textual refrain: 'Does repeating something at intervals make it more important, or less so?'" (Hollander 1988, 133). Therefore, there is explicit pressure on refrain to accrue meaning—what does it mean *this* time, and how does that compare to the others? Will it appear again, and what will it mean the next time?—what Hollander calls "the dialectic of memory and anticipation" (139). The writer may also attempt to "make structures of permutation" and "patterns of variation." Two issues he considers briefly:

> One of these is a spectrum or scale of lexical or syntactic variation, or of rhythm of recurrence (at regular or irregular intervals), along which particular applications of refrains in poems might be arrayed. Another is a sort of referential scale, with one pole at what used to be called the "purely musical" . . . the other pole would be one of optimum density of reference, in which each return accrued new meaning, not merely because of its relation to the preceding strophe (their glossing of each other), but as a function of the history of its previous occurrences in the poem.
> (135)

We'll see more of this in the discussion of passages by Terese Mailhot and Nicole Walker below.

Anaphora

Anaphora in poetry is "the repetition of the same word or words at the beginning of successive phrases, clauses, sentences, or lines" (Preminger and Brogan 1993, 73), although in lyric prose, it appears at the start of fragments or sections as well. Because of its regular appearance, it functions similarly to refrain, but with the added pressure of its insistence adding to the meaning and not simply marking time. The effect can be powerful, creating the cumulative effect of a list or catalogue, as in John Scalzi's "Being Poor," a short essay in a list format, where each descriptive sentence is of variable length and is set off as a separate fragment, but always begins "Being poor is . . ." (Scalzi 2005). The effect is a numbing sameness, of being trapped in the pattern and spinning wheels hopelessly. It can also function as a reset, bringing the piece back to a central phrase before going off in a new direction.

Rhyme

The most basic definition of sonic rhyme is two syllables that "begin differently and end alike" (Preminger and Brogan 1993, 1053). If they have identical vowel sounds and final consonants, we call that exact rhyme (bat/sat). However, unlike the Romance languages, which are limited in word endings and therefore rich in exact rhymes, English rhyme hedges its bets with a healthy inclusion of what's called slant, off, or near rhyme: similar vowel sounds and/or final consonants (bat/set). There are other types of rhyme—like visual/eye rhymes (rough, through) or nearly-always-comical mosaic rhymes (hippopotamus/top to bottomus)—but exact and slant are the most common. We're used to looking for rhymes at the end of lines of poetry, but really, they can occur anywhere within a piece.

But images and ideas may also "rhyme" in writing, recurring with some consistency, more like a motif. I think here of the riveting one-sentence prose sonnet by Diane Seuss, [I hoisted them, two drug dealers], which captures the fierce rage and anger and love of the mother of an addict, attempting to drive out his dealers, and manages to pair the violence of his C-section birth with the threat he's become. In the piece, there are several smaller moments of refrain and rhyme, like the sonic repetition of the construction "I ___-ed them," but most astonishing are the images of violent "hoisting" recurring throughout, creating the image rhyme scheme for what Seuss calls a sonnet: "I hoisted them," "I exiled them," "they picked up a stray pit bull," "after all this I want to be awake/when you lift out the kid," "I excised them, I pulled them like two bad teeth," "something in me rose up," "I excommunicated him, hoisted him" (Seuss 2021a, 67).

Rhyming—whether sonic or image—gets its power from calling attention to two or more words/images/ideas and evoking a response in the reader based on identity and difference: "The equivalence of the rhyming syllables or words [or images or ideas] on the phonic [or visual or rhetorical] level implies a relation of likeness or difference on the semantic level . . . they mutually entail each other" (Preminger and Brogan 1993, 1053). This is the main function of rhyme—the semantic function—drawing two or more rhyming instances into parallel consideration, for how they are alike or different, for how they fulfill expectations or disrupt them. There are other traditional functions of rhyme: architectural (marking key points in the structure of a form), mnemonic (rhymes stick in your memory better), closural (rhymes at endings tie things up neatly, like a satisfying punchline), heuristic (the process of selecting rhymes may aid the writer in what they want to say and emphasize or may reveal new parallels previously unconsidered), and aesthetic (rhyming for pleasure) (1060). While some of these functions are more important in verse (especially the architectural and closural functions), they are considerations in lyric essays as well. Again, Diane Seuss refers to the piece described above as a prose sonnet, and these "hoisting" rhymes occur at intervals that match the architectural rhyme scheme of a sonnet (you really have to read this piece aloud to hear how it's working), heuristically emphasize this violent motion, and create closure with "don't ask for my touch" after reciting a litany of ways in which that touch is applied violently.

Alliteration/Assonance/Consonance

These are the repetition of letter sounds, either vowel (assonance, like bat/rack) or consonant (consonance, like rack/kiss/tickle), anywhere within words in proximity to each other. Alliteration is any repeated letter or letter-combination sound, but it must occur at the beginnings of words in proximity (**b**ad to the **b**one, **cr**unchy **cr**acker). [Side note: because Germanic languages like English don't rhyme well, Old English rhymed the starts of words, which is why it's usually called "alliterative verse."] The sound effects of these three vary depending on what the writer is going for, but b and p sounds are often "bouncy" sounding, while t and k sound harsh, and r and/or l combined with other consonants sound thick and difficult in the mouth. V, z, m, and n often create a buzz or hum. Long o may sound like a moan. The writer might also simply repeat letter sounds so the reader has a heightened awareness of the music of the language, without intending a particular semantic effect. We'll see some specific instances of how these sound effects function below.

Wordplay/Homophones/ Connotation/Denotation

This type of patterning is more associative but still uses patterns of sound to create resonance between words. Here, similar-sounding or -appearing words, or even homophones, are used to slip associatively between them. The two may seem to be completely unrelated semantically until the play on words is made. For instance, in the Seuss example above, "exiled," "excised," and "excommunicated," though they are spaced apart, call across to each other because of the similarity of the words, all beginning with "ex-," as well as their placement in the identical constructions "I ex-___ed them," and because they're uncommon verbs so they stick out, all emphasizing how she's trying to cut off the addicted son who was once cut from her body (Seuss 2021a, 67). In a piece I wrote about the history of leather in perfume, I used the pronunciation of the French word for leather—*cuir*—to slide to *queer*, using the play on similar sounds to remind readers of the connection between leather and queer culture (Czerwiec 2019, 13). The wordplay may also make use of connotations and denotations to further amplify resonance, not only through associations of sound but of meanings.

Cadence/Rhythm

As opposed to regular poetic meter, lyric essays employ rhythm in more loosely expressive ways. In the early days of defending the project of free verse, Ezra Pound described it "As regarding rhythm: to compose in the sequence of the musical phrase, not in sequence of a metronome." He adds, "Naturally, your rhythmic structure should not destroy the shape of your words, or their natural sound, or their meaning" (Pound 1913). Free verse poets, without the scaffold of traditional verse forms and meters, instead matched the rhythms of their language, their patterns of unstressed and stressed syllables, to the needs of the lines' meaning, tone, action, and/or pacing.

I'm not going to go into a detailed explanation of prosody/ scansion—for that, Paul Fussell's *Poetic Meter and Poetic Form* or

Timothy Steele's *All the Fun's In How You Say a Thing* are much more comprehensive. For the purposes of this piece and to explain how cadence/rhythm apply to lyric prose, I'm going to focus on how hard stresses, and patterns of stressed and unstressed syllables, create certain effects. For how we stress the syllables in a particular word, you can look at its pronunciation key in the dictionary. We also tend to stress syntactically "important" words in a sentence—nouns and verbs, as well as anything receiving emphatic stress. If a writer puts together a grouping of one-syllable "important" words (often of Anglo-Saxon origin), the result is a clump of hard stresses that draws the ear, emphasizes the words and their meaning, and slows the sentence down. Pair those same words with dense consonants (also common to Anglo-Saxon), and the effect is even stronger. In contrast, unstressed syllables move the sentence along: if they alternate with stressed syllables, you get a trotting or heartbeat-like effect; if there are 2+ unstressed syllables between the stressed syllables (lots of latinate words or prepositional phrases), the sentence moves more swiftly. How heavily or lightly a sentence is punctuated can further intensify the effects of the cadence. Writers can use these effects to call attention to emphasized words and their meaning, to suggest a harder or lighter tone, to match the action being described with the rhythm, and to control the velocity or pacing of a piece.

For instance, in the Seuss example above, her construction of "I __-ed them" often has all hard stresses that mimic and emphasize the violence of her action: "I **ex-cised them**, I **pulled them** like **two bad teeth**" (boldface to indicate stress), where even the unstressed "like" acts as a sort of resistance to her pulling, before the language returns in force to yank at the words "two bad teeth." She pairs unstressed syllables with stressed to make the "lifting" action more forceful: "**after all this** I **want** to **be awake/** when you **lift out** the **kid**," "**some**thing in me **rose up**," the unstressed drop just before the voice lifts to stress "lift out" and "rose up" enacting the movement. And yet the forceful stresses, emphasizing the violent tone, are constantly in tension with the velocity of this one-sentence piece, like an unstoppable juggernaut, until the almost anticlimactic summary of the ending, which trails off, as if running out of steam: "so **don't ask** for my **touch** is what I'm **saying**" (Seuss 2021a, 67).

How These Elements Work Together to Create Resonance in Lyric Essays

The opening essay in Sonya Huber's hybrid collection about living with chronic pain, *Pain Woman Takes Your Keys*, "What Pain Wants," employs several of the resonance strategies described above. The essay is in the form of an anaphoraic list of sentences of varying length, each set off as a fragment, and each beginning "Pain [verb]s," which is often "Pain wants." This repetition constantly reiterates the concept of pain as its own separate agent asserting its demands on the body's inhabitant. The variations in this pattern—such as a suddenly long, complex sentence after a sequence of short, simple ones, which changes up both the syntax and the cadence, or a couple of fragments that speak across as a sequence after several discrete ones, or one that delays the verb part of the "Pain [verb]s" anaphora: "Pain, when held in place, spirals down into drill bits. . ."—thwart expectation and create surprise, much as how even chronic pain will suddenly shift and hurt in new ways. In fact, let's dig into that last example a bit more: "Pain, when held in place, spirals down into drill bits, so it has to keep moving to prevent these punctures." The sibilant consonance of *place*, *spirals*, and *bits* creates the hiss of spinning, before the hard consonants of *down into drill bits* forcefully drill down into the sound and image, before pain moves *to prevent these punctures* with their alliterative popping *p*'s. It's also possible that "in place" is meant to evoke the medical terminology *in situ*. There are rhyming images between these sentences, spaced throughout the piece: "Pain looks at you with the inscrutable eyes and thin beak of an egret;" "Pain folds the minutes into fascinating origami constructions with its long fingers;" "Pain puts its beaked head in its long-fingered wing hands in frustration and loneliness." Since this could be any bird and origami usually suggests cranes, this also makes "egret" stand out and suggests the wordplay of "regret." Pain is the pattern, though the quality of the pain, as Huber describes it, is endless in its variety (Huber 2017, 3–6).

Patterns also assert themselves in the language of this passage from Terese Marie Mailhot's "Little Mountain Woman," about the emotional abuse she experiences from the father of her child, on top of already existing emotional trauma:

I had the baby remembering the women. White women make me feel inferior, but I don't think you know how much. All you see is me killing ladybugs, how could you know the feeling. The *spite* of that feeling.

We compare hurt. I only feel dirty sometimes. I wash my face three or four times in the mirror and let the alcohol sting.

"I want to be pore-less," I say.

You tell me people have pores—that they should.

I feel dormant watching you live fuller than I can. I worry I am a cavern. I've inherited my mother's hollow stomach.

You tell me that my pain feels searing, that I'm missing four layers of skin. Your pain is an empty room. I agree that I'm mercurial and you can be dusty.

In marriage—swollen and postpartum, I stare at our bed, which is held up by books. I want to fix it. I strip the bed more often than you like. We wash the sheets. I stare at the doorway where you held her, and I see myself on the other side, a squaw. I wash my face again. Maybe, if you know, I'll feel less of this.
 (Washuta and Warburton 2019, 87)

In this passage, "feel" recurs as a refrain, with various meanings: as a passing sensation, as a body memory, to describe sensitivity and also the wish to not feel so intensely, and as a burden the author wishes she could share, to create understanding. Other anaphoric sentence starts—"You tell me," "I stare," and "I wash"—embody the themes of unequal power in this relationship and her feeling of shame/dirtiness. The sonic rhyme of *hurt* and *dirty* forces a comparison that suggests *dirty* goes deeper than her skin and can't be washed off. Because an earlier passage describes her shame at being poor, the homophone "I want to be pore-less" evokes both wanting to be free of poverty and its shame, but also to be impervious. The stinging alcohol and obsessive washing rhyme with the searing pain, as if "missing four layers of skin," and all the sibilance of *searing, missing, skin* enacts the hissing of burning flesh. And the images of both pregnancy and after—"swollen and postpartum"—repeat in "fuller" and "mother's . . . stomach," but also in the inverse as "cavern," "hollow stomach," "empty room." The obsessive washing turns to the sheets of the marriage bed she "strip[s]" and "want[s] to fix." The cadence itself—the short simple sentences, the longer ones chopped into shorter phrases with commas—create a blunt, numbed, even wounded effect that mimics the speaker's depression and traumatic, almost dissociative, detachment.

Finally, "Fish" marks the first essay Nicole Walker, previously a poet, had written, which is interesting, since my nonfiction students reading it often accuse me of having assigned them a poem, not an essay. "Fish" is a triptych in three different writing styles, scenes, and points of view—lyric nature documentary/fish ladder/close third-person; memoir/deep-sea fishing/first-person; and food writing/kitchen/second-person—and each section presents only a brief, image-based moment addressing some aspect of fish. While each section has its distinct voice, images and words echo across the essay: the straining of the salmon upstream becomes the straining of the young girl and barracuda against each other and returns as directions for making a sauce: "Strain through a chinois. Strain through cheese cloth. Strain one more time for good measure." Words like "circling," "hold," and "flesh" recur, accruing meaning. In a passage from the first section, where a female salmon is trying to climb a ladder at an electrical dam to spawn upriver, the rhythm fluctuates between the tumbling flow of the water and the short, choppy progress made by the fish:

> . . . She directs her body against the current.
> All the roe she had to hoe.
> Eggs lined up in her tubes. Red roe. Follicular. Funicular. She looked at the cables of fire streaming above her. Follicles polishing those little apples.
> Apple of her eye. Her silver skin turning apple-skin—ripening. Dying. Water polishing the concrete to a smooth, slippery, no holds, no nook, no rub step.
>
> (Walker 2013, 1)

Here, "current" evokes both the increased pressure of the dammed river and the electricity and both echoed in the "cables of fire streaming." The play on "hard row to hoe" gets presented as the sonic and eye rhyme of "All the roe she had to hoe." Like the salmon funneled to climb the fish ladder, "Eggs lined up in her tubes. . . . Follicular. Funicular." The exact rhyme and syllabic stress, as well as the wordplay of those two words, emphasize both the reproductive drive of, etymologically, eggs lined up, but also suggest the folly of this funneling of the salmon on the ladder. The "Red roe" become "little apples," the "apple of her eye" that drives her maternal instinct, and the reddish speckled appearance her "apple-skin" takes on at this reproductive stage of "ripening." And yet the loving "polishing" of those egg-apples becomes the "water polishing the concrete" to a fluid, unstressed slipperiness, to a no-no-no nothing, hard step-stresses that are negated, hastening her death.

In the early days of *vers libre* and prose poems, when Modernists were defining and defending their project in the nascent pages of *Poetry*, Amy Lowell in "Vers Libre and Metrical Prose" described the continuum between pure poetry and pure prose (with vers libre and metrical prose placed somewhere in the middle) as being a matter of "wave lengths" (picture a sine wave) and that the "length and sharpness of the curve," the "rate of return," determines where on the continuum it falls (Lowell 1914, 215–16). Although she is talking about rhythm and cadence, her model works to measure the rate of return of all patterning in a piece. One of Gerard Manley Hopkins sonnets—like "God's Grandeur," with such lines as "all is seared with trade; bleared, smeared with toil; / And wears man's smudge and shares man's smell" or the "Sirens" chapter of Joyce's *Ulysses* would have a wave pattern like a tachycardic heart about to burst; the wave pattern of directions for installing your printer would practically flatline. Lyric essays would fall in the middle of the continuum, possibly closer to the "pure poetry" or lyric end. This is not to say that a particular wavelength, such as the 440Hz middle "A" orchestras tune to, distinguishes a prose poem from a lyric essay from a flash nonfiction piece. But it is useful to think about the "rate of return" in the pattern of resonances of each if trying to define its category is important. This concept gets echoed by D.I. Masson in 1960 in his "Thematic Analysis of Sound in Poetry" when he suggested strength or intensity of patterning could be quantified in terms of "bond density" (cited in Preminger and Brogan 1993, 1176). And there may even be variations in wavelength or density between lyric essays: for instance, I arranged the passages above—by Huber, Mailhot, and Walker—from less to more dense occurrence of resonance, from a wider to a tighter wavelength or rate of return. That I think this is apparent from these passages indicates there could be a general measure or comparison of the level of lyricism, though "more lyric" shouldn't be construed as "better." Rate of return could explain why brevity is often a feature of lyric essays: while there are book-length lyric essays (not a sequence made of smaller sections), sustaining such a densely compacted rate of return over hundreds of pages is exhausting!

A denser rate of patterning in lyric prose creates a slower, but richer, journey for both writer and reader. In fact, this fantastic voyage through an experience crafted from language is so lush, *The New Princeton Encyclopedia of Poetry and Poetics* can't help but wax rhapsodic in this passage uncharacteristic of its usually drier prose:

> In general, movement in thought is forward, toward completions. . . . Sound patterning [I would expand this to include any patterning] complicates this movement: slows it, often; changes sentence rhythms, prose emphases; makes us dwell on words we should otherwise, perhaps, attend to less; multiplies our awarenesses, our kinds of awareness . . . all these relate to one another, affect one another, orchestrate the flow of thought. As readers of verse we must learn how to listen, how to receive fully, how to move susceptive through the landscapes of thought and feeling.
> (Preminger and Brogan 1993, 1182)

My point is, by studying and understanding the functions and effects of these different patterning techniques, and the strategies for using them, and by just listening with an ear attuned to them, readers and teachers and writers of the essay learn how the *lyric* contributes to the lyric essay and how writers employ these techniques to orchestrate and choreograph how we move through the landscape of the text, not only reading, but listening and feeling, as we dance along behind the lyre.

The Resonance of Lyric Essays, or Lyre, Not Liar

On Resonance: *Lyric*

I shall write about resonance. Here's the truth: when I first heard the resonance, I sang out loud. The song burst forth, I could not stop it. And now that I've admitted singing, I shall admit this: what sounded forth was jubilant, rhapsodic, astounding—whatever is the opposite of calm.[1]

Resonance is what Judith Kitchen insists with her declaration against D'Agata: "to be lyric there must be a lyre. . . . The lyre, not the liar."

Resonance of origins, lyric, Orphic, endorphic. Strike a chord, an accord of notes, denoting and connoting, a word-chord of word-play, proliferating.

This is how to begin. This is how to begin again. This is how to wear your refrain with a difference. Don't space your rhymes too far apart for the ear to hear. Don't amplify your alliteration, lest you write like the slut you are so bent on becoming.

Resonance begins with sacred theft, then a gift, and ends with a bargain. Apollo's sacred herd returned; the fine, Hermes's invention,

---

[1] This essay contains riffs/reworkings of bits of Lia Purpura's "Autopsy Report," Jamaica Kincaid's "Girl," Wallace Stevens's "Thirteen Ways of Looking at a Blackbird," Timothy O'Brien's "The Things They Carried," Shakespeare's *A Midsummer Night's Dream*, and Brian Doyle's "Leap," and borrows its form from John Scalzi's "Being Poor."

a lyre from a liar; then, offered to Orpheus. Tortoise shell strung with entrails. Hollowness that hits you in the gut so hard even Hades himself will trade with you, your lyric skill for your silent sylph of a wife.

Resonance is how we learn by rote: the English rote, small lyre the bard strums in time with the mnemonic rhymes to firm them in the mind.

We will not be discussing whether "that really resonated with me" so let us never speak of it.

Resonance: at all the "Thirteen Ways" essays, the bawds of euphony cried out.

Resonance, the rosin on the bow creating texture in the text, the drag across the strings, resinous. The bow bows to no one.

A bard, a bawd, a bird, traveling throughout the piece, a Chanticleer strumming his Oo-De-Lally.

Resonance as aural tagging of significant words, signifiers spray painted with bright sound—semantic underlining, a sonic highlighter.

Songbirds decorate their nests with scraps of resonance, some spectacular bits, but beneath it, nested patterns of sound provide the structure.

Language interpretation happens in the left hemisphere of the brain, yet musical sounds are interpreted by the right hemisphere. Resonance as the harmony of the spheres. When the tonic and fifth of a chord are played perfectly in tune, their sound waves average to create an audible ghostly third—invisible scrim, thin meniscus vibrating between. Both sides are listening intently.

We carried the resonance itself. We marched for the sake of the march, simple writers, soldiering with our pens, because it was cadence, it was anatomy, and the resonance was entirely a matter of posture and carriage, the resonance was everything—and for all the mysteries and unknowns, there was at least the single abiding certainty that we would never be at a loss for sound to carry.

Resonance, what carries, bears us back, each thread, each spoke of speech starting from the same wheel hub.

Resonance the rhythm, the soundtrack below the action, the beating heart, the pulse along the vocal chords, an unbridled galloping faster and faster until the beat is beat back. A stick in the spoke. Stop. Restart.

While refrain means to bridle, restrain a thought or feeling, the lyric refrain is freeing, unbridled, a body leaping across the expanse of the page.

Resonance a sound re-sounding, to reverberate, to echo, the sound patterning a system by which we echolocate through the essay's space.

Resonance as sonar. In English, sound comes from Old Norse *sund*, which also means swimming, a body in water. As well as a body of water bordering the sea. A body made mostly of water in a body of water, dissolving borders (between writer and reader, between word and speech), where the ear (whose?) amplifies sound, sounding the depths of an essay. It shall be called "Bottom's Dream" because it hath no bottom.

My music theory teacher taught us sound is founded on three conditions: a source, a medium through which sound travels, and a receiver. Thus, the tree falling in a forest koan, resolved. Timber/timbre a relationship based in sound. Do you hear what I hear? Without you, dear reader, no resonance.

Resonance: I saw Doyle do it and I saw Kincaid do it, and I saw Purpura and O'Brien do it and I hang on to that.

Image Alt-Narratives: Deep-Diving, Mutating, and Chaining

On the Image: Traditional

I've argued in several places that lyric essays progress or move in ways alternative to narrative. One strategy is by manipulating how images function in lyric mode, developing or morphing them in ways that substitute for narrative or logic. In helping me work through these ideas about image, Karen Babine asked, Is it the images themselves or is it the language creating these connections and substitutes for narrative/linear progression? That's an interesting question and one I'd be happy to see discussed more. A distinction exists: "Nevermore" is a resonant language refrain that does not describe an image; when M. H. Abrams describes his "mirror" and "lamp," they are metaphors to help us understand his concepts but contain no music. But my instinct is to say, in the lyric essay in particular, they can't be separated, because the writer crafts the images for the reader out of language chosen for its density of resonance, and recurrence of image often is paired with refrain of sound, syntax, and/or structure in the language.

Diana Wilson echoes this dialectic, non-narrative movement of language and imagery, specifically tying it to the lyric essay in her excellent "Laces in the Corset," a discussion of the "Structures of Poetry and Prose that Bind the Lyric Essay." In it, she describes most of her examples she studies in terms of synonyms for resonance—repetition, recurring, reflexive, connective, retrospective-prospective. However, it's important to distinguish that she focuses on *visual* resonances of images and the authors' dance between representation of that image and presentation/reflection on it, rather than on *sonic* resonances. Wilson also shares my frustration that non-narrative/nonlinear lyric essays often get labeled "disjunctive" when we need to pay attention to the *connective* tissue the authors have intentionally crafted: "a careful study of lyric essays will reveal a cornucopia of connectors and structures rooted in both poetry and prose ... binding the fragmented imagery ... bringing order to apparent literary chaos" (Wilson 2015).

When critics point to "nonlinear" or "disjunctive" in lyric writing, it seems like what they mean is the way in which the lyric disrupts *time* (something I discuss in more detail in the essay "Lyric Time"), because lyric writing does create connections or progressive movement in other ways, sonically and imagistically. But with lyric writing that prominently features the deep development of one image or the evolution of an image throughout a piece, there can be "junctions" that are not narrative—what may seem like "leaps" of juxtaposition may actually be associations across which we can trace the process of mind. James Longenbach in his fantastic *The Art of the Poetic Line* gets closer to this problem when he examines a prose poem by John Ashbery, arguing for how the prose subverts our expectations of narrative. He says of Ashbery's prose poem,

> The passage looks like prose, but it invokes the narrative logic we associate with prose while at the same time dismantling it. . . . [T]he narrative links are suppressed, and the real pleasure of the passage lies in the way it leaps. . . . Rather than fulfilling the expectations aroused by narrative logic, the passage foregrounds the disjunctive movement we associate more readily with poetry and in particular with lineated poetry.
> (Longenbach 2008, 89–90)

I would disagree with Longenbach on the grounds that he seems to be implying non-narrative equals disjunctive, and this is not automatically the case. Even Longenbach is making assumptions about both prose and poetry, narrative and lyric, distinctions crucial to articulating how the image functions in a specifically lyric way that makes a lyric essay, well, lyric. These functions, by which the image creates alternatives to narrative or linearity, include deep-diving, repetition and/or mutation, or metamorphosis by means of image-chaining.

This progressive movement might not progress so much as deepen or expand, focusing on a single image that accrues meaning as the mind contemplates it. Brian Doyle's "Leap," while it contains other images (falling, fire, pink mist), chooses as its imagistic throughline "hand in hand" because that is what allows him to keep his faith despite the horrific events of 9/11. After reporting accounts of eyewitnesses, including several who saw the couple leap, "hand in hand," Doyle tries to pray but admits (with a stunningly complex pileup of lyric adjectives) "I keep coming back to his hand and her hand nestled in each other with such extraordinary ordinary succinct ancient naked stunning perfect simple ferocious love." The "hand in hand," which he acknowledges might have been a conscious choice or might have been reflex, transforms for Doyle into an image of prayer—"Their hands reaching and joining are the most powerful prayer I can imagine, the most eloquent, the most graceful"—and in fact the only prayer he can manage: "I hold on to that" (Doyle 2003, 129–31). This expansive engagement or deep dive with an image also functions in long-form lyric essays, such as the color blue in *Bluets*, with all its historical, aesthetic, and personal associations, or the blank journals Terry Tempest Williams's mother left behind in *When Women Were Birds*, an image through which Williams explores ideas of absence, emptiness, and purposeful silence.

But the lyric writer also repeats images with variations, creating a motif or motif system through which images mutate or evolve, repeating with variation to drive the piece. Deborah Tall, in the intro to the *Seneca Review*'s apocryphal 1997 issue, asserts such images may replace narrative in the lyric essay, that "the stories it tells may be no more than metaphors," an etymological acknowledgment of metaphor's transitive state, of how the image is "carried over," transformed from one thing to another (Tall and D'Agata 1997). I've already talked about this with regard to resonance but wanted to highlight it a bit more here as a lyric technique, a way to structure a piece in an alternative to narrative—rather, the writer traces an evolution of thought through an evolution of images, thinking with images that morph as the writer's thoughts do.

For examples of how this progression or evolution through motif system works, I'll recall a few texts I discuss elsewhere. In *Holy the Firm*, Dillard asserts early on "Nothing is going to happen in this book" (Dillard 1977, 24). There's no real plot or linear movement, but this short book-length lyric essay progresses associatively via various image permutations on the motif of fire: the book opens with "the god of today" rising like fire over the Puget Sound before we get the famous passage of Dillard reading the fictionalized biography of Rimbaud titled *The Day on Fire* by candlelight when a moth gets stuck in the candle and its body becomes a sizzling wick. From there, the moth-wick image is transformed into Julie Norwich (the name a play on the fourteenth-century mystic and anchorite), a local girl whose face is badly burned in a small plane crash, and then into a seraph, an angelic being all wings and eternally aflame with love for God. These images come together at the end, when she concludes, "I am moth; I am light. I am prayer and I can hardly see" (65), and yet all we can do is marvel and suffer, on fire with love, because "the world without light is wasteland and chaos" (72).

We've also seen this progression by motif system in the prose sonnet by Diane Seuss, [I hoisted them, two drug dealers], with the images of violent "hoisting" that recur throughout, creating the image rhyme scheme for what Seuss calls a sonnet: "I hoisted them," "I exiled them," "they picked up a stray pit bull," "after all this I want to be awake when you lift out the kid," "I excised them, I pulled them like two bad teeth," "something in me rose up," "I excommunicated him, hoisted him" (Seuss 2021a, 67). I've also made this argument about Walker's "Fish" where, while each section has its distinct voice, images and words echo across the essay: the straining of the salmon upstream becomes the straining of the young girl and barracuda against each other, and returns as directions for making a sauce: "Strain through a chinois. Strain through cheese cloth. Strain one more time for good measure." These as well as images evoking or using the language of "circling," "hold," and "flesh" recur, adding to the sense of struggle and violence when humans and fish interact (Walker 2013, 1–3).

There's also progression through images I would call image-chaining, where instead of various permutations of the same image, the images progress through metamorphoses, much in the sense of Ovid, where one image bleeds into the next, into the next, in a sequence of seemingly unrelated images connected by thought. I overtly called attention to this technique in my prose heroic crown of sonnets *Sweet/Crude*, where the image/language of the last sentence of one "sonnet" becomes transformed into a new image in the next "sonnet" to show the interlocking issues facing the Bakken region during the oil boom/bust: the Cannonball Sea becomes Lake Agassiz becomes a lake of oil beneath the Great American Desert of the plains, becomes the desert of the Middle East, becomes foreign, becomes flyover country, becomes "what lies beneath you," becomes aquifers and agricultural land poisoned by injection wells, becomes spills and fracking accidents, becomes violence in the man camps, becomes boom and bust, becomes explosions of trains, becomes explosions of growth and traffic, becomes drug and human trafficking, and so on (Czerwiec 2019, 78–92).

I've also noted this effect in a passage from the first section of Walker's "Fish," where a female salmon is trying to climb a ladder at an electrical dam to spawn upriver:

> . . .She directs her body against the current.
> All the roe she had to hoe.
> Eggs lined up in her tubes. Red roe. Follicular. Funicular. She looked at the cables of fire streaming above her. Follicles polishing those little apples.
> Apple of her eye. Her silver skin turning apple-skin—ripening. Dying. Water polishing the concrete to a smooth, slippery, no holds, no nook, no rub step.
>
> (Walker 2013, 1)

Here, the image-chaining or metamorphoses happen in quick succession. The play on "hard row to hoe" gets presented as the sonic and eye rhyme of "All the roe she had to hoe" followed by the row of "Eggs lined up." And like the salmon funneled to climb the fish ladder, "Eggs lined up in her tubes. . . . Follicular. Funicular." The "Red roe" becomes "little apples," the "apple of her eye" driving her maternal instinct, and the reddish speckled appearance her "apple-skin" takes on at this reproductive stage of "ripening." And yet the loving "polishing" of those egg-apples becomes the "water polishing the concrete."

We also see this chaining in the first paragraph of Hanif Abdurraqib's essay on dance marathons, Black dancing, and the Soul Train Line,

"On Marathons and Tunnels" from *The Little Devil in America*, where he sets the scene imagistically before moving into the history. Here is the whole paragraph:

> When the thick fog of exhaustion set in on a room, it was desire that kept a dancer's body upright. When the desire wore off, it would be another dancer, pulling their partner up by the arms. In the photos from the Depression-era dance marathons, women sometimes appear lifeless in the arms of their men. In some photos, men lean their resting bodies on women who have their backs arched, standing and trying to support the dead weight of the person affixed to them.
>
> (Abdurraqib 2022, 5)

Desire/exhausted upright dancer becomes dancer held up by partner's arms, becomes women appearing "lifeless" in men's arms, becomes men's "dead weight" supported by women.

And yet, before we go too far, I want to transition from these examples of images in lyric essays to consider how the images are being used in explicitly lyric ways that make these essays lyric essays. The problem is that aside from Wilson, there isn't a lot on the image in the lyric essay—most just point out lyric essays use a lot of descriptive imagery, or they may talk about hybrids incorporating visual elements as part of the text. Therefore, we must turn to the poetic theory and craft underpinning this in order to discuss how images function lyrically to reveal a specifically lyric process of mind.

Ellen Bryant Voigt also distinguishes between narrative and lyric modes of progression: "Flannery O'Connor said, '[I]n a story something has to happen. A perception is not a story.' But perception is precisely the lyric poet's gift, and the lyric poem may be, as Charles Olson said, 'one perception immediately followed by another'" (Voigt 1999, 102). Because the lyric essay is not a story, it must develop in alternate ways. Voigt explains how, besides using syntactic strategies, one avoids narrative by "structure[ing] the information through the lyric, or musical, devices of juxtaposition and . . . repetition" or by "creat[ing] a formal and syntactical context that pushes emphasis away from the event. Pattern supplants suspense" (111–12). While these patterns may be sonic, they can as easily be imagistic, and both poets and writers of lyric prose often pair these lyric strategies to move the text forward.

This patterning, but with development, also works for motif systems. I again call attention to Hollander's work on refrain, which, he argues, creates circular and/or back-and-forth movement different from narrative/plot and which also creates reader engagement and suspense: What does it mean *this* time, and how does that compare to the others? And what will it mean next time?—what Hollander calls "the dialectic of memory and anticipation" (Hollander 1988, 133, 139). These theme-and-variations, but using a motif that evolves through various permutations, allow the image to accrue meaning as the piece progresses, revealing how the author's thoughts about the image and its meaning have also progressed.

This connection of image to thought has a strong history in poetics. Early lyric theorist John Stuart Mill asserted the Romantic position that "'The poetry is not in the object itself,' but 'in the state of mind' in which it is contemplated . . . the poetry must be true not to the object but to 'the human emotion'" (quoted in Voigt 1999, 57). As a result, the image represents not so much the object, but the object as perceived by the subjective artist. Voigt projects this history even further back:

> For the contemporary lyric poet of classical OR Romantic affinity, then, the most useful function of the image would seem to be less imitation than dramatization. That is, image can supply not only what the writer-as-camera uncovers in the empirical world, or what the writer-as-ecstatic isolates and articulates from the whirl of the individual psyche, but the moment when both are fused in objects seen, heard, smelled, and rendered with human response still clinging to them.
>
> (63)

Voigt solidifies this argument of the image as representation of the writer's process of mind, down to the syntactic level, in her essay "Rethinking Adjectives." She starts by reminding us that one of the main elements of the lyric—the image—is a noun: "If the noun is fact, then the verb is movement, change, mutability. In the choice of a verb, the poet selects from the possible relationships among separate nouns and further directs with parallel or subordinate verb action" (Voigt 1999, 38). From there, Voigt contends with the adjective, and its more recent troubled history in the lyric, in order to argue *for* the adjective as a lyric strategy. She points to the Modernist distrust of Romanticism's overuse of adjectives because the adjective is subjective; in contrast, Eliot idealized his elusive "objective correlative," while Pound exhorted poets to "Use no superfluous word, no adjective, which does not reveal something . . . use either no ornament or good ornament" (40–1). However, Voigt argues that adjectives, *because* they're subjective, are crucial to the lyric: "Pound, Eliot, and others were correct in linking ornament to the subjective: it is precisely their location IN the subjective that makes adjectives indispensable to Plath's lyric, just as the meditative or discursive poem needs its nouns to chew on, the narrative its verbs to convey events in time and their consequences" (43). This is not to say she's arguing for an excessive pileup of adjectives, a more-is-more approach. On the contrary, the adjective can serve precision because "syntactically, the adjective provides enormous advantages of economy, since its family includes articles, comparatives, and participles" (44), which can help fold definition, simile, and even multiple parts of speech into less words, thereby limiting description. To return to her title in the sense of rethinking adjectives, how they can show the writer's thought, she argues that as a result, adjectives can also add complexity and amplify possible meanings and even contradictions in a poem (45–51). She concludes, "In short, adjectives not only annex precision and clarity, for more exact meaning, and add nuance and resonance, for evocation of emotion; in their amplifications of tone they acknowledge the poet's subjective presence in the poem. In fact, the adjective perhaps springs more directly than any other part of speech from the lyric source" (51). By extension, how the image is presented directly reflects the poet's thinking, lyrically represented.

Ann Townsend agrees the image is a representation of the process of mind in her essay "A Mind for Metaphors" in *Radiant Lyre*: "Mental wandering, the mind at play, and the seemingly accidental associations that emerge from wandering: these are the tools we use to create the collage that corresponds to our lives. In this way, both metaphor and contemplation arise from the same fertile ground" (Baker 2007, 227) The word "seemingly" is doing a lot of work in that sentence, implying the associations made by metaphors aren't accidental at all. I would extend this to the mind that pairs certain adjectives with certain nouns in images and any description. And if those associations aren't accidental, then they're not irrational or illogical either—metaphor explicitly creates a connection between two things. In a now-famous mini-masterclass on metaphor delivered via Instagram, Ocean Vuong attests,

> [Figurative language is] my favorite literary device because it reveals a second IDEA behind an object or abstraction via comparison. When done well, it creates what I call the "DNA of seeing." That is, a strong metaphor (Greek for "to carry over") can enact the autobiography of sight. For example, what does it say about a person who sees the stars in the night sky—as exit wounds? What does it say about their history, their worldview, their relationship to beauty and violence? . . . How we see the world reveals who we are. And metaphors explicate that sight.

But, Vuong asserts, this is a nonlinear associative logic rather than a linear argument logic: "a metaphor is a detour, but that detour better lead to discoveries that alter/amplify the meaning of what is already there" (Vuong 2020).

Which gets us to process of mind as a way of thinking *with images*, again showing how those "seemingly accidental associations" are no accident. Pound, in "Vorticism" and his early critical arguments on the image and Imagism, claimed, "The 'image' is the furthest possible remove from rhetoric" (Pound 1914, 463). *But what if it's not?* What if how the image is deepened and explored, or how it develops and evolves, can make Townsend's associations or the thoughts of Voigt's writer visible? What if you can think with images? Even Wimsatt and Beardsley, who coined the idea of "process of mind" with their critical work on Wordsworth and Coleridge, acknowledged a "qualitative progression" of images in "The Affective Fallacy," by way of Winters: "Winters has shown, we think, how there can be in effect 'fine poems' about nothing. There is rational progression and there is 'qualitative progression,' the latter, with several subtly related modes, a characteristic of decadent poetry. Qualitative progression is the succession, the dream float, of images, not substantiated by a plot" (Wimsatt and Beardsley 1949,

49). They both mean this pejoratively, as insubstantial nonsense. But given their acknowledgment of the powerful feelings evoked by image/metaphor, why can't a "succession . . . of images" have its own qualitative sense of progression? Why would it need to be attached to either plot/narrative or rhetoric? The answer is, *it doesn't*. "This, too, matters, says non-narrative nonfiction," says Joni Tevis, "which creates meaning through accretion" (Tevis 2013), which is why this strategy appears to such effect in the lyric essay.

In fact, the lyric essay uses this nonlinear lyric strategy to involve the reader more directly in co-creating meaning. It invites us, the readers, to think alongside, to make these connections for ourselves. Again, Vuong: "A metaphor that actually invites you to put the book down, think on it, absorb it, before returning. A good metaphor uses detours to add power to the text." In explaining that in Tibetan Buddhism, "the world and its objects are pure perception," and how this informs his phenomenological approach to metaphor and figurative language, Vuong says metaphor invites us into this perception, this process of the author's thought: "Buddhism explains this by saying that, although a text IS thought, it does not THINK. We, the readers, must think upon it. The text, then, only curates thinking" (Vuong 2020).

This is particularly powerful—and important—in the lyric essay, because when we see prose, we expect narrative or linear development. When that expectation is thwarted or subverted, we are tempted to dismiss a piece as merely disjunctive. But what we should be doing instead is trying to determine how, in the absence of linearity, the text is curating a thought process—and one of the most effective methods of doing so is through image alt-narratives: an emblem on which to meditate deeply, a leitmotif that leads us like cairns along a trail, or a relay baton passing ideas between us.

Pushing Up Daisies: Three Image Alt-Narratives

On the Image: *Lyric*

I. PUSHING IN

The image opens with the sun, cauldron of morning, that starburst pattern of petals and bracts: daisy. Day's Eye, lens through which we see, focus, and understand a mind's working. Think of Ocean Vuong's thread on metaphors, his vision of starlight as a night sky with exit wounds. Roripaugh's disaster of asters. What kind of mind's eye would see that way? How we link ideas with images, blink them together like eyelids, paired like spectacles we wear to see anew, sunglasses for stargazing, our stare aslant.

II. PUSHING OUT

Fresh as a daisy, a white-and-yolk-yellow ovation for new beginnings and births, even motherhood, how images mutate, expanding to enfold new forms, evolve: for instance, Freya's flower as symbol of fertility revised for the veiled Mary's immaculate conception, the unblemished fruit of her womb, vulva inviolate. For those plucked too soon, the gods covered graves of babes with daisies, the very image of innocence. Purity, though not always positive. In a bouquet, daisies convey innocent love and the ability to keep a secret. And though she swore never to tell, and though Vertumnus told her his unwanted advances were innocent fun, that he'd never pluck her too soon, the nymph Belides morphed into metaphor, translated to a daisy to escape his narrative.

III. DAISY CHAIN

Daisy, give me your answer, how you translate to an Americanism for first-rate, as in, *you're a daisy if you do.*

How daisies, like thoughts, may be strung together to form a chain, a crown, though this involves a minor violence, a splitting of stems to thread another flower stem through, creating a connection from one image to the next, forging a sort of progression, a succession of links, a loop.

A lariat, from *la riata*, a rawhide or hemp rope noosed in a large loop, to lasso the idea above the image and truss it up. A loaner term from Spanish that enters our language when Mexican herders encounter southwestern ranchers.

We called them vaqueros, cattle drivers, cowboys who become a cultural stereotype, herding their words, their Americanisms, law unto themselves, loner who nonetheless breaks a trail for us to follow into their wild west.

Doc Holliday was an educated gentleman, a loner known for a way with words, not a cowboy but known for fighting them, known to have said "then you're a daisy" when a cowboy at the OK Corral claimed he'd gun Doc down.

And though it's a scene invented for *Tombstone*, after Doc easily defeats Johnny Ringo, leaves him pushing up daisies, Val Kilmer closes the loop, why he does declare in a cartoonish drawl, "You're no daisy at all."

Using Poetic Forms in Creative Nonfiction

On Poetic Forms: Traditional

While hermit crab, collage, and braided forms are popular in literary nonfiction, one of my favorite techniques to teach is using traditional poetic forms to structure flash nonfiction. I myself came to nonfiction after a long stint as a poet who studied, taught, and wrote in verse forms and so was naturally drawn to hybrid forms. Lyric essays, prose poems, and flash all seemed like fun ways to move between genres. But I discovered that while lyric prose borrows heavily from prose forms (scene, parable, joke, fairy tale), this borrowing doesn't often happen in reverse. Although Brenda Miller and Suzanne Paola, in their textbook *Tell It Slant*, coined the term "hermit crab essay" (Miller and Paola 2005) for an essay that adopts the shell of another form—to-do list, want ad, recipe, etc.—verse structures haven't been embraced as fully. I do want to note Miller has made forays in this direction, both in a panel discussion on "The Poessaytics of Form" at NonfictioNOW in 2015 (Czerwiec 2015) and in a piece I will discuss later. But as a craft technique, there has been only one other panel at a national American conference that specifically engages with this strategy, the NonfictioNOW 2018 panel "The Essay as Unstrung Lyre: Prosody in Nonfiction Forms" (Czerwiec 2018).

Using verse forms, with their ready-made scaffolding, can be a real boon for writers of flash prose. Because of their inherent patterning, verse forms can be used either to reveal patterns in the content or to impose order on what seems like chaos. When I teach this technique, I like to distribute a handout outlining a few verse forms and their formal elements and structures. I've been using the sonnet, haibun, sestina, and pantoum, but any verse form is fair game. (The Poetry Foundation's website at poetryfoundation.org can be searched for form explanations and examples, and writersdigest.com has a "List of 168 Poetic Forms for Poets.") I assume many of the students aren't overly familiar with prosody, so I keep the discussion of form light and not too in-depth—basically, what kinds of content these forms and their elements pair well with, what formal features they're known for that could help us organize and give structure to our flash prose (number of lines becomes number of sentences, stanzas become paragraphs, refrains, rhetorical elements, possibly rhymes), and which elements are optional.

Next, we read examples of flash prose written using a verse form as a scaffold. For the sonnet, I use an example from my prose sonnet cycle *SWEET/CRUDE: A Bakken Boom Cycle* (Czerwiec 2019, 78–92), which uses the form to craft arguments about the issues surrounding fracking in western North Dakota—each piece is fourteen sentences long, with a volta (turn), and I do not rhyme the ends of sentences in this piece (though I have elsewhere). Diane Seuss reinterprets the form differently in her memoir-in-sonnets, *frank: sonnets*, where each autobiographical moment or scene is rendered in fourteen lines of prose, though the number of sentences varies, and which include other sonnet features such as voltas or rhymes in the form of rhyming syntactical or lyrical gestures. In her hybrid book-length text *Dandarians*, poet Lee Ann Roripaugh incorporates haibun, short lyric prose pieces that periodically crystallize into a haiku-moment:

> . . . like a bird who doesn't even wake while the Madagascan moth slides a plundering tongue under its eyelids, secretly drinking away all the bird's tears.
>
>   This phlebotomized
>   and thief-parched heart has no tears
>   left over for you.
>   (Roripaugh 2014, 91)

María Isabel Alvarez's "Strawberry Girl: A Prose Sestina" repeats six words—*whispers, dirt, gloves, smoke, recreational, remembering*—using the sestina pattern but at the ends of sentences. The form allows Alvarez to portray the unhealthy patterns of behavior that ultimately destroy a family:

> . . . Knead the soil and fertilizer as if it were flour between your fingers, pull the weeds from their clutch the way your husband pulls his lungs in with smoke. This isn't supposed to be therapeutic; this isn't supposed to be recreational. This is what they call *remembering*.
>
> All you want to do is practice remembering. At sixty-eight, your mind begins to fade until it only whispers. As you knit baby-pink booties, needles tangled like chopsticks, your husband lectures that your activities should be "less stagnant, more recreational." Your senses have warped, so when he speaks your ears eat his words and your eyes taste their resentment; you want nothing from this life except to sleep in the quiet of the dirt.
>
> (Alvarez 2016)

And Brenda Miller's "Pantoum for 1979" uses the advance-and-retreat narrative pantoum form to reveal patterns of behavior, each four-line stanza adapted to a four-sentence paragraph, allowing herself variations in the repetitions:

> I'm twenty years old, barely an adult, my belly flat—though inside that belly a baby is growing. Or not a baby: a *something*, a cluster of cells lodged in the fallopian tubes. In a few weeks I'll be in pain, like a penknife stabbing again and again. But for now I'm just a girl in a broke-down Toyota, moving her few belongings into a room in a big red house on a hill.
>
> Not a baby, I'll remind myself later, just a cluster of cells, lodged where it didn't belong. I must have found this house from a tacked message on a bulletin board on campus.
>
> (Miller 2016, 52)

After discussing the forms and examples, I have students either bring a piece of short nonfiction they've been working on or freewrite from a choice of prompts. Then I ask them to consider what form might pair best with their content (argument or problem/resolution = sonnet, distilled moment = haibun, obsessive = sestina, circular narrative = sestina or pantoum). Since picking the six sestina words can be tricky, I'll often provide lists of six words with the invitation that they are welcome to cheat or substitute.

While nonfiction students often are skeptical or anxious about engaging with verse forms, this exercise results in fantastic work. As I found when writing poetry in verse, keeping the left brain occupied with structural elements frees the right brain to make inventive and surprising connections it might not otherwise make. I absolutely allow myself and students to cheat with the form—it's supposed to be in service to the content, not governing it—but the verse structure provides additional ways to think about organizing content while boosting its lyricism.

(R)Evolution Pantoum: Play with Your Food

On Poetic Forms: *Lyric*

After Brenda Miller's "Pantoum for 1979"—and, really, after Brenda in so many ways

Narrative, even in creative nonfiction, leaps forward, circles back in circuit. But 1990s Utah, desert no dessert—as at other creative writing programs, the choice an *or*: fiction or poetry, narrative or lyric. A limited menu, prix fixe, the occasional à la carte visiting writer, or nonfiction workshop taught by a dabbling faculty, and always, always, as a square meal of narrative. When offered, though, those classrooms stuffed, writers starved for it, nonfiction the neutral field on which we fed.

Utah, as elsewhere, fed us into fiction or—like me—to poetry. Then Brenda Miller was afforded, forded, foraged the first dissertation in creative nonfiction—a foretaste—though her degree notes none of this. At her defense, I recall the classroom stuffed, us writers starved for it. We hungered to see what she'd do next.

After Brenda broke the seal, things blurred a bit. Dawn Marano cultivating a taste for nonfiction at the University of Utah Press[1]; in course, Utah adding nonfiction to the spread, hiring Robin Hemley as a dedicated position. We hungered for what came next, couldn't know how Robin and Nicole Walker (also there, studying poetry) would nurture NonfictioNOW.[2] But that was then, and even then, lyric essays slow curing in Nicole's cranium.

And not just Utah—other programs (Ohio, Nebraska, Eastern Washington, though not Iowa) added nonfiction to the spread. Phillip Lopate spread from teaching fiction to nonfiction, edited *The Art of the Personal Essay*[3]; *Creative Nonfiction*, *River Teeth*, and *Fourth Genre* a pop-up of publishing. Deborah Tall coined the fusion cuisine "lyric essay."[4] Dinty W. Moore begat *Brevity*.[5]

Still, *River Teeth*'s subtitle is "A Journal of Nonfiction Narrative," wouldn't break *Beautiful Things* tiny milkteeth for fifteen years[6]; the selections in Lopate's anthology firmly in narrative's maw. At best, they ruminated through meditations, assayed and essayed a bit less logical. Even Dinty, in *The Best of Brevity*, claims his nascent mag considered only the compressed narrative.[7] Soon, however, his concept of flash omnivorated.

But writers ruminated through meditation toward less logic, more lyric. Work labeled flash, prose poems—at *Quarterly West*, when we didn't know what to do with them, we published these delicacies as whatever the author preferred; the anthology *In Short* (Judith Kitchen and Mary Paumier Jones)[8] proffered them in all their chimerical glory. By Y2K it was clear the possibilities omnivorated. While *Tell It Slant* (Brenda Miller and Suzanne Paola)[9] presented a craft table of memoir and journalism, it also offered a taste of lyric essay.

Despite being labeled poets, writers—Elissa Gabbert, Maggie Nelson, Claudia Rankine—were crafting delicacies no one knew what to do with. We devoured them like gathering breadcrumbs to trace a path, gorging on those leaping, circular forms. After *Tell It Slant*, Rose Metal Press (Abigail Beckel and Kathleen Rooney)[10] added a leaf to the craft table, made a groaning board of those lyric essays and braids and hermit crabs. If it seems like women nourished much of this work—they did, they do—I don't know what it means but it sustains me.

Devouring those early poets-turned-essayists, I could trace a path for my own work, as I gorged on Doyle's *Leaping*[11], on Lee Ann Roripaugh's haibun and zuihitsu.[12] I browsed poetic genres and conventions, bending them to prose. I read for sustenance, this stuff by women, to realize, astounded, spun around, that my favorite Annie Dillard book, *Holy the Firm*, is a book-length lyric essay, an evolutionary leap forward in 1977.[13] But, like anything, the writing aged ahead of the critical work explaining *how*.

Bending Genre (edited by Nicole Walker and Margot Singer and featuring a lot of Utah expats)[14] tried, and succeeded, at feeding us some answers. Even Lopate argued "The Lyric Essay" in his update *To Show and to Tell*[15] (spoiler: he's agin' it). All that writing, finally nibbling at *how*. In 2015, NonfictioNOW had a couple panels on hybrids; in 2018, a smorgasbord.[16]

And yet, in 2020, my grad students at the University of Minnesota argued the lyric essay (spoiler: they're agin' it), not for inability to digest but fed up, glutted on it. Utah now offers a feast of "fiction, nonfiction, poetry, digital writing, hybrid and other experimental forms, [and] book arts."[17] In 2018 at NonfictioNOW, invited to the table, I presented on a hybrid panel[18] (mostly women) on poetic forms imported into nonfiction and cited Brenda, present in the audience, got to thank her for setting that table. This is not to say all is sweetness: recently, Ander Monson addressed distaste for lyric essay in NEA grant judging[19] (spoiler: they're agin' it).

Creative writing programs and syllabi cellars at *Assay*[20] and elsewhere now offer a feast for teaching and studying, an entire palette of genres for every palate. Far from the food desert of the 1990s, us gone undernourished, the limited menu prix fixe poetry and fiction; the only sips of nonfiction, narrative. Despite this, narrative nonfiction still gets the grants, the agents and advances, the main entrée on the buffet (I prefer to make a meal of hors d'oeuvres, am always eyeing what's being circulated on the platters). But as we see, even narrative circles back, awaits the great leap forward.

Notes

1 https://www.dawnmarano.com/.
2 NonfictioNOW webpage. http://www.nonfictionow.org/the-board.
3 (Lopate 1995).
4 (Tall and D'Agata 1997).
5 Brevity Magazine webpage. https://brevitymag.com/about-brevity/.

6 "Beautiful Things" webpage, *River Teeth Journal* https://www.riverteethjournal.com/online-content/beautiful-things.
7 (Moore 2020).
8 (Jones and Kitchen 1996).
9 (Miller and Paola 2005).
10 Rose Metal Press webpage. https://rosemetalpress.com/about-us/.
11 (Doyle 2003).
12 Roripaugh, Lee Ann. *Running Brush*. Website. https://runningbrush.wordpress.com/.
13 (Dillard 1977).
14 (Singer and Walker 2013).
15 (Lopate 2013).
16 *Assay* blog: Conference Reports https://assayjournal.wordpress.com/category/conference-reports/.
17 University of Utah Graduate Creative Writing webpage https://english.utah.edu/graduate/creative-writing.php.
18 (Czerwiec 2018).
19 (Monson 2021).
20 *Assay* blog: In the Classroom https://www.assayjournal.com/in-the-classroom.html.

The Four Temperaments of Creative Nonfiction

I'm going to advocate for expansive, associative writing in creative nonfiction essays and essay collections, by way of an association I made between a review by Beth Alvarado and a piece by Diane Seuss, which I read in close succession, and by way of an association Diane Seuss's piece makes with Gregory Orr's "Four Temperaments and the Forms of Poetry."

First, Beth Alvarado alerted me she was including my essay collection *Fluid States* in a collective review/craft essay in *River Teeth* on the shape or effect of different ways of grouping essays together in a book. In reading her review essay, I was struck by an issue she raised, about "horizontal" versus "vertical" development. (She means across full collections, but I think the issue is also relevant in sequences or individual essays.) She describes "diagramming" or "mapping" the development of various collections and contrasting them as either a "horizontal" or "lay of the land" development of theme, or a "vertical mining" that "deeply and narrowly" drills into a specific topic. Pleased with this model, she says, "I like the idea of some kind of spatial arrangement that is not dependent on the linearity of chronology or on developing a long-form narrative, which may imply cause/effect relationships and may limit their design and oversimplify their purpose." Instead, she says,

> I saw distinct advantages to collections in which writers explore various topics *and* explore the various *possibilities* of how the essays might work together. As such, these collections attempt to enact the variety of their subject matter. And, just as the essay is **expansive** within itself when it encourages writer and reader to make connections among things that might seem, on the surface,

disparate, so then is a collection of such essays also **expansive** when it experiments with its own literary form, creating an organic and self-reflective work of art.

(Alvarado 2021, italics hers, boldface mine)

I want to pause here to explain how Alvarado's description of horizontal versus vertical differs from other creative nonfiction craft discussions that use those terms. In Bascom's "Picturing the Personal Essay" (Bascom 2013), Ballenger's "The Narrative Logic of the Personal Essay" (Ballenger 2018), Stephanie G'Schwind's "The Artful Placement of Needle Against Album" (G'Schwind 2013), and Sue Silverman on horizontal and vertical plots in her craft book *Fearless Confessions* (Silverman 2009), "horizontal" and "vertical" are primarily discussed in terms of the tension between the more grounded movement of time or narrative (horizontal) and meaning or reflection (vertical), both of which all those authors assert are necessary in creative nonfiction. It's also important to note all these sources privilege creative nonfiction working in or with narrative mode. In contrast, Alvarado is including alternatives to narrative mode and thinking about how content and form are used either to drill down into a topic (vertical) or to explore multiple associative topics expansively (horizontal), as something that has a shape or might be mapped. In fact, at one point, she describes my collection as "cone-shaped," beginning in a tight focus and ending with a zoomed-out expansive focus, and Sloan's *Dreaming of Ramadi in Detroit* as collage-like, "spatially arranged with texture" (Alvarado 2021). In this instance, Alvarado's conception of this movement has more in common with Jane Alison's *Meander, Spiral, Explode*. After reading Alvarado's piece, I kept coming back to this idea of "mapping" essays or essay collections in terms of horizontal or vertical development. I kept trying to pin down how this would work. And while I liked this idea, I found myself thinking her term "expansive" might ultimately be more useful.

The same week Alvarado's piece posted, I had ordered a copy of the new *Poets & Writers* because Diane Seuss had an article in it which I did not want to miss. Haply and happily, "Restless Herd: Some Thoughts on Order—In Poetry, In Life" dovetailed with the issue Alvarado had raised which was still haunting the back of my mind. In it, Seuss pulls from a key poetics craft essay to speculate on how it could apply to the shapes of collections:

In "Four Temperaments and the Forms of Poetry," Gregory Orr proposes that all poets enact one of four core temperaments in their work—story, structure, music, or imagination. Story and structure, he writes, are limiting impulses. Music and imagination, conversely, represent an impulse for limitlessness. Each of us is in our sweet spot within one of the four temperaments. To grow as a poet, Orr suggests, is to walk across the lane and integrate one of the opposing temperaments...

I'm wondering if the same could be said for a book manuscript. If your poems tend toward the limiting impulses of story or structure, might you arrange the manuscript to spark musical or imaginative energy, steering clear, for instance, of overt linear order? If you're in the music or imagination camp, could you try shaping your book with an eye toward structural and/or narrative coherence?

(Seuss 2021b, 45–6)

Seuss is talking about poetry book manuscripts here but raises some of the same issues: limiting impulse (vertical?) development versus limitlessness/expansive (horizontal?) movement. However, instead of what Alvarado says about it seeming to be an either/or, Seuss, via Gregory Orr, calls for exploring both, one as a counterbalance of the other, to create useful tensions and to develop the writer as well as the writing. Therefore, I temporarily would like to table the discussion of vertical versus horizontal in favor of exploring how limiting and expansive impulses function. Since I have the Orr essay Seuss cites, I went back to reread it.

To give a little more explication of Orr's argument, he outlines the four temperaments of poetry as follows:

- **Story:** pulling from Aristotle, Orr defines this as primarily action and event, and story may equal drama: "What is essential to story is that there be at least two centers of energy, two poles of awareness around which the conflict can organize itself." He explains that this may be two characters, or the poet arguing with the self, or the self at odds with the world (Orr 1996, 271–2).

- **Structure:** pattern making in either closed or open structures. Orr asserts that structure is not imposed on a piece, but primary to it, an essence (272–3).

- **Music:** the qualities of syllables, syntax, sound effects "as they interact to create the poem's aural and rhythmical structure." Orr claims, "Music in poetry is irrational; it works directly on the emotions, regardless of the purported content of the language" (274). [Interesting aside: despite music usually being equated with lyric, Orr here associates music not with Apollo's lyre but with Dionysius's flute.]
- **Imagination:** abstract and/or concrete imagination. Orr says that it is difficult to define because "an individual poet's imagination moves in ways so peculiar and particular to him or her. . . (275). How then does a poem governed by the imaginative temperament overcome its own centrifugal impulses and finally cohere?" He says the answer is the poet's "train of thought" (277). [It's this "train of thought" where we could reassert Alvarado's vertical versus horizontal movement—more below.]

In drawing alignments among these qualities, Orr asserts, "It is essential to recognize that the four temperaments form another pattern. Story and structure are *intensive* in their impulse; music and imagination are *extensive*. Story and structure concern limits and correspond to our desire for and recognition of the role of law. Music and imagination concern our longing for liberty, the unconditional and limitless" (270).

I've created a model to help us visualize Orr's temperaments:

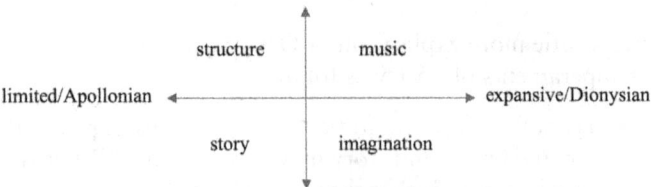

Orr then draws implications for the writer for how these temperaments might be used to create balance, tension, or even growth:

> Although each of the temperaments is capable, in and of itself, of creating the unity we call a poem, for a poem to have the stability and dynamic tension that comes of a marriage of contraries it must fuse a limiting impulse with an impulse that resists limitation. (270)

He continues, "it should be added that combining two impulses from the same column can be fatal." Music + Imagination risks incoherence because it "makes it almost impossible to create closure, to constellate a wholeness," while Story + Structure by themselves can come across as "hollow," "unconvincing" (270–1). However, once a writer understands where their own temperamental tendencies are grounded, there are two possibilities for growth:

> The first is to go further into the gift, but such a decision carries with it the risk of narrowing as well as the promise of deepening. The second direction is to expand. Such an expansion can be understood as the poet's struggle to nurture and develop the other temperaments in such a way that their energies and constraints enrich his or her poems.
>
> (277–8)

Again, Orr—like Seuss—is talking about poetry and is suggesting that while a poet's strength might reside within one or two particular temperaments and might grow by deepening that strength, the best work often pushes itself to expand into one or more of the other temperaments.

But this got me thinking: I agree with Orr and Seuss in their encouragement for poets to incorporate a temperament from an opposing impulse, in order to bring balance, tension, and amplification, to their work. This concept is quite helpful, but not all that radical to the discussion of poetry and poetics; however, it's causing much perplexity in creative nonfiction circles. Why does expansive/associative/horizontal development seem so alien?

I think it goes back to the evolution of creative nonfiction pedagogy and craft I describe in my prose pantoum essay. Both narrative and lyric modes have been around in poetry for millennia; all four temperaments which Orr proposes have been explored in various combinations. But for creative nonfiction, with its origins in journalism and fiction pedagogy, the emphasis has long been on narrative mode, with Bascom et al.'s vertical theme or with imagination/assay mode as the only ways to expand, both limited by allegiance to the verifiable truth or to speculative "perhapsing" (Knopp 2009) (unless you want to eschew facts and go the way of D'Agata). Only relatively recently have the expansive/associative elements been incorporated, even celebrated, or the concept of "structure" redefined in either more poetic or more open, intuitive ways (cf Alison), or craft essays written and published to articulate how this might be accomplished.

So how does this apply to creative nonfiction? I'm hoping this discussion might be imported to help give a framework to articulate how expansive practices are shaping essay collections. Lyric and/or hybrid essayists are already doing this, so the following is especially beneficial for discussing those forms or for writers of traditional narrative looking to expand. Therefore, may I please (re)introduce you to The Four Temperaments of Creative Nonfiction:

Temperament of Poetry	Temperament of CNF	Explanation
Story →	Narrative mode*:	Because Orr somewhat conflates story and drama, in the context of CNF, this could include both traditional narrative elements, as well as interior conflict
Structure →	Structure:	In CNF, structure has long meant narrative structures and only more recently has included other structures: hermit crab essays, braids, adapted verse forms, etc. Also, the analogy to my take would be that formal CNF relies on structure for lyric patterning; lyric essays NOT ALSO written in a form rely on lyric patterning for structure
Music →	Lyric mode:	Similar to music, but including both patterns/resonance of sound and image
Imagination→	Assay mode:	Orr's "both abstract and concrete imagination" and "train of thought" translate to assay mode's tracing of the author's process of mind, both analytical *and* associative

*For these modes, please see Karen Babine's "Taxonomy" (Babine 2020) for a more thorough explanation.

FOUR TEMPERAMENTS OF CREATIVE NONFICTION

These temperaments translate pretty well from poetry to creative nonfiction. At this point, we can return to Alvarado's discussion of vertical versus horizontal movement. I kept trying to make it work across all of the temperaments, and it didn't seem to fit, but I didn't want to give up on it. Finally, I realized where it fits best is in that last temperament, assay mode. Here, a concrete, analytical train of thought could represent a vertical movement, drilling down into a topic, getting closer to the story of it: topic as narrative, as character. In contrast, a more abstract, associative train of thought could represent a more horizontal, expansive movement, one interested more in lateral developments of theme rather than a specific topic. Revising the model of Orr's temperaments to apply to creative nonfiction would look something like this:

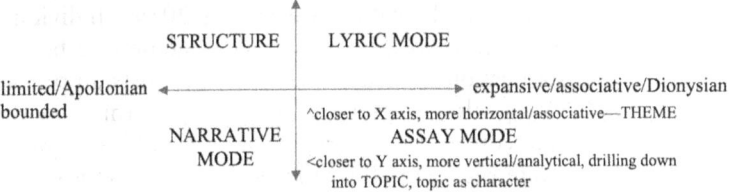

To illustrate, let's apply this to some collections Alvarado's piece discusses. I'll start with my own, since it's the one I'm most familiar with (forgive the crude graphics):

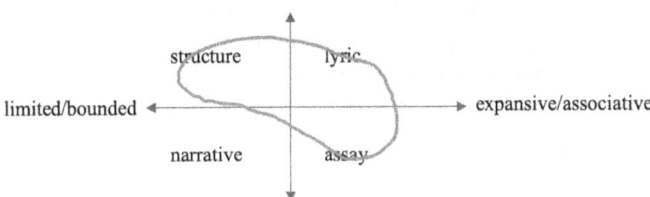

Heidi Czerwiec's *Fluid States*

My map is kidney-shaped, weighted top and right on the chart, because it's a collection of lyric essays in various forms. Its assay mode is largely associative: though individual essays/sequences dig into particular topics (perfume, fracking), and topics are loosely connected by the theme of fluidity or fluid situations, they range widely. Narrative is not a strong impulse in the collection. While the individual forms tend toward structure/boundedness (haibun, prose crown of sonnets), the overall tendency is toward expansive/

lateral/horizontal movement, what Alvarado describes as a "cone" expanding from a point to a wide, panoramic view.

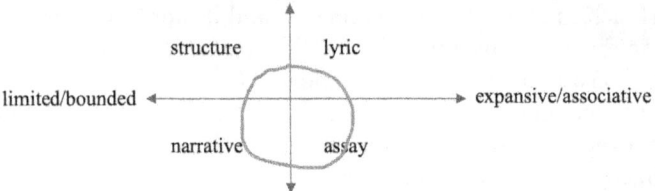

Esmé Weiiun Wang, *The Collected Schizophrenias*

Wang's collection is an off-center circle, fairly balanced, but tending more toward narrative and a deep dive into the topic of schizophrenia and mental health care (Wang 2019). Individual pieces do use some structures, such as story structures or braids, but the book is a memoir-in-essays and, as such, resists an overall narrative arc. Wang also employs some lyric patterning in the service of trying to convey the experience of a mental break, but it is not a driving impulse. Again, the collection is fairly balanced but tends somewhat more toward the vertical.

So, what's the effect of this? Wang's is more balanced. Mine risks expanding out of control because of the emphasis on associative assay mode and lyric mode—my use of structure may somewhat ameliorate this, yet it's probably why Alvarado struggled with seeing how it worked as a collection.

To look at a few more models:

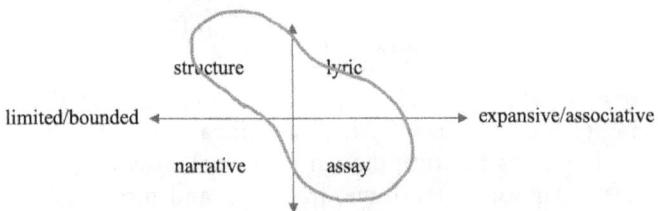

Chelsea Biondolillo, *The Skinned Bird*

Biondolillo's map reminds me somewhat of a left-leaning peanut. While there are some narrative threads woven throughout this collection of essays, narrative is not the primary temperament. Instead, these pieces explore various formal and visual structures, and focus on recurrent topics and themes: birds, their songs, silence, migration (and other patterns of behavior) (Biondolillo 2019). As a result, along with structure, both analytical and associative assay modes are emphasized, as well as lyric in terms of image patterning. This collection's use of recurrent terms as both topics and images is both vertical and expansive/associative.

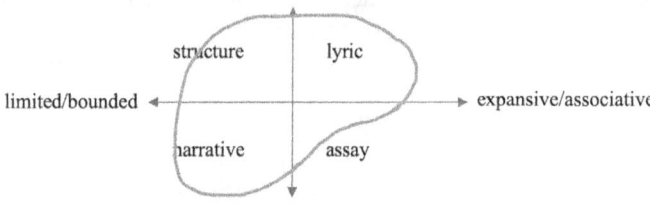

Diane Seuss, *frank: sonnets*

And because I couldn't resist, and as homage to one of the prompts for this craft essay, I've mapped Diane Seuss's recent book, the memoir-in-prose-sonnets *frank: sonnets* (Seuss 2021a). This one also looks like a kidney but is weighted top and left, a vertical flip of mine. Her collection, like mine, emphasizes structure (the prose sonnet form) and lyric mode (sound/image/language patterning). But where mine falls more under assay mode's associative/analytical train of thought, Seuss's memoir is, by virtue of being a life story, more tied to narrative (though not strictly chronological). This collection is fairly balanced as well, between the vertical focus on one life and the expansive/associative movement through various memories.

But lest you think I've forgotten my original evangelism, I want to return to a push for more associative, expansive creative nonfiction. A few days after Alvarado's piece posted, in an online discussion thread on the pleasures and perils of associative thinking in creative nonfiction, Nicole Walker and I and some other nonfiction writers, mainly those known for more lyric writing, continued to latch on to Alvarado's idea of horizontal, expansive development. I post about a recent craft piece I've written on lateral moves in the lyric essay. Nicole says, "My dream is to make this kind of associative, horizontal rather than vertical thinking a more exalted form of writing." Someone responds, "I think we're on the edge of that wave." Many others enthuse, "this thread gave me LIFE. Very much an associative thinker." Or even "how do you know if you're an associative thinker?"

It appears lyric and hybrid essayists are already doing this—some intuitively and some with an awareness of these discussions of mode and structure—though it's always useful to be able to articulate these choices in a conscious way. Therefore, it seems like the main benefit would be to writers of more "traditional," narrative nonfiction. Perhaps these maps might be useful as a heuristic device, both in the classroom to visualize how an essay or group of essays is working modally and by writers to get a sense of the movement and/or limitations of their work. But this map wouldn't have been possible without Orr, so my point is that by importing craft from poetics, it might benefit and give us expansive ways of understanding creative nonfiction and essay collections.

Revisiting Annie Dillard's *Holy the Firm*

Today is November 18.

Recently, I found myself rereading Annie Dillard's metaphysical text *Holy the Firm* (Dillard 1977), a brief book that set me on fire to become a writer. In it, she describes rereading James Ramsey Ullman's *The Day on Fire*, a novel about Rimbaud's brief life that set her on fire to become a writer. As she's reading by candlelight, one of the moths circling the light gets stuck in the candle and becomes a wick, burning brightly (16–17). While it was this passage I was looking for, to parallel it with Virginia Woolf's "The Death of the Moth" for a student assignment, I ended up sitting there and burning through the whole book.

Holy the Firm is a slim volume—only sixty-five pages of text—published in 1977, after she spent two years holed up like an anchorite on the Puget Sound, with a cat used as a spiritual prop, much like Christopher Smart's Jeoffry. "Today is November 18" (25), she tells us in the first section, "Newborn and Salted," where she sets her scene and establishes the themes—birth/death, the elementals of salt, sea, and fire—that will resonate throughout the book. The moth passage appears only a few pages in and is transformed in the second section, "God's Tooth," first into Julie Norwich (the name a play on the fourteenth-century mystic and anchorite), a local girl whose face is badly burned in a small plane crash, and from there into a seraph, an angelic being all wings and eternally aflame with love for God. In the last section, Dillard describes struggling with faith, a baptism in Puget Sound, and a substance said to be the most elemental of elements, in touch with the Absolute, called Holy the Firm. She concludes, "I feel the wine . . . I am moth; I am light. I am prayer and I can hardly see" (65), and yet all we can do is marvel and suffer, on fire with love, because "the world without light is wasteland and chaos" (72).

Because I've been thinking and writing about the lyric essay, I have the flash of insight that *Holy the Firm* is a book-length lyric essay, in the same company with Maggie Nelson's *Bluets* and Heather Christle's *The Crying Book*, though preceding either of those. So many features of the lyric essay are here: the resonant elemental images of salt and sea tied together by birth and baptism, fire and the flaming moth transformed to burnt girl and seraph, the struggle with God and the lesser gods of time we seem abandoned to, echoing in the anaphoric phrase "the god of today." Dillard flat-out asserts her aversion to narrative and her allegiance to lyric early on: "Nothing is going to happen in this book. There is only a little violence here and there in the language, at the corner where eternity clips time" (24).

The phrase "lyric essay" isn't coined until (apocryphally) 1994 and described in 1997 (Tall and D'Agata 1997). But as Amy Bonnaffons reminds us in "Bodies of Text: On the Lyric Essay":

> Of course, essayists were writing lyrically long before D'Agata and Tall and the *Seneca Review*; [D'Agata's] anthology's transhistorical focus proves as much. Furthermore, D'Agata never claims to have been the first person to utter the term—just to institutionalize it. The term caught on partly because it described something people were already doing, that had only lacked a unifying generic label. The fact that they continued to do so once that name existed, perhaps more visibly, should not be viewed as an argument that anyone needed the permission of D'Agata or of *Seneca Review* to create such work.
>
> (Bonnaffons 2016)

And there are moves to retroactively claim key texts as lyric essays: Sei Shōnagon's *The Pillow Book*, John Donne's meditations in his *Devotions Upon Emergent Occasions*, Gertrude Stein's *Tender Buttons*. Even Dillard's book was originally classified to be shelved with nonfiction nature writing or as philosophy.

But what does it mean to go back and label a work as "lyric essay"? Obviously, there's the temptation to claim certain authors and texts for Team Lyric Essay. More importantly, though, Joanna Eleftheriou asserts in "Is Genre Ever New? Theorizing the Lyric Essay in Its Historical Context" that naming the lyric essay made it possible to theorize about it and its features (Eleftheriou 2016). And both Bonnaffons and Eleftheriou point to the Jackson and Prins critical anthology *The Lyric Theory Reader*, which includes a section that frames the genre debate over the lyric between Ralph Cohen (genre is descriptive and transforms over history as cultures and their needs/values do) and Jonathan Culler (genre is normative and stable across history, which is why we know a genre when we see one) (Jackson and Prins 2014, 53–77).

It's not yet settled where and how lyric theory applies to the lyric essay. But in trying to theorize about the lyric essay and its features, applying the label to prior works helps us trace a lineage, to look at what techniques earlier practitioners were using as they felt their way through writing alternatives to narrative nonfiction. Techniques we're still using: in Dillard's case, resonances of image (god, fire, sea, salt) and sound (anaphora, echo, and wordplay) and allusion— an associative, nonlinear structure that begins and ends at the end of November but circles and spirals as if tracing a labyrinth. The way in is the way out.

As I finish writing this, it is November 20. As Dillard finishes *Holy the Firm*, she says, "Today is Friday, November 20" (59).

Ekphragrance

Often, creative nonfiction engages with memory. Yet despite the fact that no sense is more immediately linked to memory than smell, from a writerly perspective no sense is more neglected as we learn to flex our descriptive abilities. For lyric essays, where lyric description of embodied experience is a hallmark, this sense requires more attention and strengthening. I came to writing about smell through attempts to write about perfume, and my hope is to offer some of the tools I learned during this process to help other writers develop this ability.

Smell was the first of our senses, the mass of olfactory material budding atop our nerve cords eventually blooming into a brain. The center of this liminal, limbic system—the amygdala—not only produces emotional responses to stimuli but also connects the senses. I inhale: physical odor molecules huffed to the back of my nasal cavity, behind the nose's bridge, where microscopic hairs called cilia sweep them into absorbent mucosa containing receptor cells. Just eight molecules trigger a receptor impulse, sending a signal to the olfactory nerve that lies only two synapses apart from my amygdala. If a mere forty receptors out of my five million fire up, I smell something. And I smell it directly, unedited, unmediated (Ackerman 1990, 10, 13). Perhaps this is why my eyes close or go unfocused when sniffing a scent deeply—because sight is unneeded, even distracting. Most emotional long-term memory is thus coded by scent, across time and distance.

But it took me a while to recognize this power and attempt to employ it. As a professor, I would try to engage my students' intellects through their senses. When I taught Modernist Literature, I used a multidimensional approach so they could comprehend the radical aesthetic departures of the art of this period. In order to understand attempts to represent multiple character perspectives simultaneously in Eliot and Woolf and Joyce, we studied Picasso's Cubist paintings and listened to Stravinsky's polyphonic compositions; to learn about absurdism in Kafka, we heard Mahler's First Symphony—the third movement with "Frère Jacques" played as a minor-key dirge until interrupted by an oompah band—and looked at slides of Dadaist lobster phones and fur mugs.

The last time I taught, this class coincided with the start of my perfume obsession and research, and it occurred to me I didn't know what these Modernists smelled like. What, if anything, could this sense teach us about the people of this period? Our sniffing sessions helped round out our perception of the shifting gender roles: garçonnes, those young women, raided not only men's closets but their scents, and perfumes followed suit. Since smoking and drinking in public were barely tolerated, fragrance gave cover, cloaking women in heavy tobacco and boozy scents.

Using smell to understand a moment is one thing; writing about it is another. Immediately, I ran into problems. Through researching perfume, I realized I needed to learn to incorporate descriptions of smell into my writing. Perfume has been linked with language since the days it rose as prayer *per fume*, through smoke from burnt offerings and incense. But why write about something you cannot experience along with me? As perfume blogger Denyse Beaulieu laments, "Write about perfume, and you'll be caught between your own limitations, those of your readers and the fact that, usually, they won't have the fragrance on hand to compare their impressions with yours" (Beaulieu 2012, 157). Your own limitations begin with the limbic system itself, olfactory messages sent straight to the brain, undiluted by language or conscious thought. Even once processed, the physiological links between the smell and language centers of the brain are weak. While smells might lodge in the memory, "without language, without a name and a context, even the most familiar smells can be fugitive, teasing things" (Harad 2012, 25). Plato gave smells no names, claimed they could only be defined in terms of other smells which, while disappointing, I recognize in our habit of describing a smell as "it smells like ___."

This issue is compounded by the difficulty of conveying your experience to another, especially when people persistently believe smell is subjective. Critics Luca Turin and Tania Sanchez strongly assert smell is objective—it's the language that's subjective: "Mostly, we don't smell things differently—we interpret and describe them differently" (Turin and Sanchez 2009, 51). In this way, we're returned to the arguments Voigt and Vuong make that I discuss in "Image Alt-Narratives": how we interpret and describe something demonstrates a lyric way of thinking and tells us more about the perceiver—in this case, more about the smeller than the smell.

However, while our sense of smell is quite precise, it can be difficult, if not impossible, to describe a scent to one who hasn't smelled it. Fortunately for perfume enthusiasts, Beaulieu says, "the very nature of the object seemed to attract a particularly literate community of amateurs" (Beaulieu 2012, 156). And perfume—or what Turin calls "chemical poems"—has a language and an approach worth examining in order to understand how we can apply these descriptive techniques to writing about scent and memory.

When I started writing about my experiences with perfume, the perfume blogs provided a place for me to compare my perceptions. As I worked my way through samples—loving some, hating others, ambivalent about many—I practiced my descriptions, first taking notes based on my own experiences: what I noticed, what notes I recognized, reactions. Then, I would compare against reviews posted in online blogs and discussion boards, learning the name for the dusty, bitter herbal note I kept smelling (vetiver), or why so many florals carry a not-unpleasant funk (indoles—fecal/decay notes that lurk beneath a good jasmine), or those powdery, soapy notes so popular in old vintages (iris and/or aldehydes, what most call "old-lady" scent). Some early entries from that time: CB I Hate Perfume's *I Am a Dandelion*, "sharp green but with a sickening sweet note like the sanitizer at the veterinarian's office"; Estée Lauder Private Collection, "flowers and cut stems in a power suit—reminds me of Lucille Bluth"; Serge Lutens's *A La Nuit*, "a singular jasmine note shooting through a woodsy base, like a winter moon through bare trees—Mozart's Queen of the Night."

Comparison—what something smells like or of, of what it reminds you—is a natural and a useful starting point. As you can see, my descriptions above include "smells like" language. But descriptions of smell can be more compelling if they move past that, into synesthesia and metaphor. Because smell is processed in the limbic system prior to language, at the amygdala which makes connections between the senses, a smell is an inherently synesthetic object. And we can use that sensory overlap to overcome the gap between smell and language. Once we try to put a smell into language, we interpret it, translate it into the descriptions of other senses and even arts, endowing smells with shape, color, sounds, textures, personalities, and narratives. To return to the example of scent, there's a whole category of perfumes called "green"—*Vent Vert*, Chanel N° 19, *Silences*—a vegetal effect achieved with the herbaceous resin galbanum. A perfume might be rounded (*Chamade, Diorissimo*) or angular (*Bandit, Laine de Verre*), plush (*Cuir de Russie*) or dry (*Vetiver Extraordinaire*). It could be mouth-watering (*Shalimar*), spicy (*Tabu*), or bitter (*Scherrer No. 1*).

Others move beyond synesthesia and into metaphor, even elaborate extended ones, granting perfumes personalities. One of my favorite characterizations is of Caron's *Narcisse Noir*, by Patty of the Perfume Posse blog, who says "this tramp drags the orange blossoms around through the dark mud of crazy . . . [it] doesn't waste a second trying to look innocent, sane or normal, and I find the lack of pretense refreshing" (White 2012). Luca Turin describes Creed's *Love in Black* as iris that "just suffered a disfiguring car crash" (Turin and Sanchez 2009, 360). And some extend the characterization into a full narrative. In Turin's appraisal of *Insolence*, he says,

> It feels like a seventies action-movie poster, with a helicopter hovering over a burning building to the right, two cars jumping off a pier in the middle, a girl in a white dress being lifted out of a swamp in a guy's arms at left, and an erupting volcano in the background. . . . There is something reckless, irreversible, cataclysmic about pressing the spray button (I should note he gives this scent his highest rating, 5 stars). (313)

Blogger Barbara Herman literally makes the metaphor literal: "A great perfume . . . invites us to shore up all of our senses, to borrow their metaphors to make perfume's story more legible, its cinema more visible" (Herman 2013, 6).

So let's try to make scent more visible. There are two main ways to apply these techniques to writing about memory, one the inverse of the other: you can start with the memory and try to remember its associated smells, or you can start with smells and let them lead you into memories. If you have a particular memory or time period that you're working with, you may already have a scent in mind you can smell to mine for more memories. You could also work to remember or else research what scents would have paralleled the same period—what foods were present? what scented products (perfume, aftershave, hairspray) would the people in the memory have been wearing then? what other smells might have been in the air (cigarette smoke, motor oil, pine needles, dog fur)? Locating and re-sniffing these scent sources might round out those memories, revealing new aspects.

The difference between writing specifically about perfume and using smell to write about memory is one of purpose. Given the olfactory cortex's role in the limbic system, how it governs us, it cannot be detached from subjective memory and emotion. With perfume, that can be a problem, since perfume writing represents the difficulty, if not impossibility, of delivering an identical experience to all, of an objective correlative of scent. We ultimately cannot be forced to experience a scent other than how our animal brains have each individually developed to encounter it. But for memoir and personal essays, scent is merely an access point for memory—whether or not the reader can "smell" what you're describing isn't as important as the memory it gets us to. And as the sense most directly plugged in to memory, it would be a shame to let smell go undeveloped. If you're working in lyric essays, the need to develop your descriptive powers for this sense is especially crucial. As perfumer Edmond Roudnitska says, "the sense of smell is ... entry into a special universe infinitely rich in signs" (Roudnitska 1977).

Structures of Thinking: Structure, Syntax, and Form in the Lyric Essay

On Structure: Traditional

Too often, "lyric" gets reduced to subjective feelings and emotions, and I'm afraid I myself have been overemphasizing lyric's musical functions, but these ignore how subjective experience also includes *thought*—that lyric writing can think through its subject but makes its argument with patterned language. In "Strike a Chord: The Lyre That Makes the Lyric" and "Image Alt-Narratives," I've talked about how this works on the word level in the sense of imagery and sound effects. But here, I want to zoom out a bit to discuss how lyric writing uses structure and form, *for lyric purposes*, to demonstrate its thinking, what Wimsatt in his critical work on Romantic poets traced as "process of mind." More recently, Jane Alison, in her excellent book *Meander, Spiral, Explode: Design and Pattern in Narrative*, claims, "Our brains recognize and *want* patterns. We follow natural patterns... [and we] invoke these patterns to describe motions in our minds, too" (Alison 2019, 22). Specifically, I want to argue that there is such a thing as lyric grammar and syntax, that these show the writer thinking lyrically at the sentence level using structures to contain both meaning and music simultaneously, and that in lyric prose these structures actually become more, not less, important. Lyric thinking, composed of these patterns, may shape itself into various forms, but ultimately, the lyric essay is a structure of thinking, a way of functioning on the page and in the ear, not a form.

Lyric Structures: Syntax

For patterns on the sentence level, we should start with syntax. There's no one better than the late poet and critic Ellen Bryant Voigt for discussing syntax as a structure of thinking, as well as of music, and how it functions in the lyric—Jane Alison herself, in her excellent book on alternative narrative forms, cites and acknowledges Voigt. While we tend to think of syntax and the sentence as the province of prose, because of how we encounter it *linearly*, Voigt's work is crucial to understand how syntax functions *lyrically*, which could be invaluable for writers of the lyric essay. Voigt's concern is obviously poetry, and her interest is in distinguishing the lyric from the narrative mode. In *The Flexible Lyric*, she claims lyric mode can "create a formal and syntactical context that pushes emphasis away from the event. Pattern supplants suspense" (Voigt 1999, 111–12). It is this focus on patterning that makes writing lyric.

While Voigt began thinking about lyric syntax in her earlier craft book, her arguments culminated in her formidable end-of-career *The Art of Syntax*. In it, she is able to demonstrate how syntax functions as a structure of thought in the lyric while also doing double-duty as a medium for music in the language. Both music and speech involve theme (deep structure/grammar) and variations (infinite combinations/syntax): "In language as in music, repetition—whether lexical (the same words) or grammatical (the same function for the words) or syntactical (the same arrangement of the words)—also marks phrases or chunks. As in music, these units can also be grouped into even larger chunks, paragraphs, or stanzas, to form astonishingly elaborate but comprehensible structures" (Voigt 2009, 11). We can store the information of these phrases/chunks by means of recall stimulated by such patterns as parallelism, inversion, branching, and others. Lyric writing exploits the variety of syntactic patterns available to create its "unique human utterance," selecting the pattern that best demonstrates/represents/conveys the unique perception and the unique process of thought of its author. But Voigt goes further and explicitly connects these choices of syntax in lyric writing to music, quoting Frost: "A sentence is not interesting merely in conveying a meaning of words. It must do something more: it must convey a meaning by sound" (43). In this way, Voigt argues syntax in the lyric consists of syntactic meaning (meaning with regard to role in sentence, relationship to other words, context) + syntactic rhythm (emphasis that certain parts of speech receive in a sentence, which affects music/cadence). Therefore, how a writer selects and arranges syntactical patterns will necessarily affect syntactic rhythm:

> Two rhythmic systems, then, by which to "control the intonations and pauses of the reader's voice," as Frost would have it. In one hand: the power of artifice, the management of the line, and the poet's handy opportunity to tap the reader's hunger for pattern . . . and therefore song. In the other hand: rhythms of syntax, which are embedded in the language itself and used unselfconsciously as we translate the world before us: the rhythms of thought. . . . Only in poetry . . . can we find both systems working at fullest capacity.
>
> (77)

I would argue this is also true of prose writers working in lyric mode. Though they have mostly dispensed with the poetic line, their close attention to the simultaneous patterning of language and sound pushes their prose into lyric territory. Fortunately, Voigt and others have also addressed this, in the form of the prose poem, which helps get us closer to applying these concepts to the lyric essay.

James Longenbach, in *The Art of the Poetic Line*, states: "We are used to thinking of prose poetry as writing that sacrifices lineation in order to partake more readily of certain aspects of prose: our attention shifts from line to sentence, and syntax must hold our attention without the additional direction of line (or meter or rhyme)" (Longenbach 2008, 87). While I agree with his main statement, I contend that his parenthetical addition is wrong. Meter and rhyme have not disappeared altogether: strict meter may loosen to cadence or rhythm, and rhyme corresponds to resonances of sound and/or image. Therefore, in lyric prose (whether prose poem or lyric essay), repetition of sound and image (see my essays "Strike a Chord" and "Image Alt-Narratives") are equally as important as—and, as Voigt argues, are often inextricable from—syntax. In fact, this patterning is simultaneous. As Voigt puts in in her title essay "The Flexible Lyric," "Even prose poems need rhythmic patterns and sonic construction, only depending more heavily on syntax than does metrical verse" (Voigt 1999, 150). Counter to the popular misconception that free verse and prose poetry are total free-for-alls where the poet just writes whatever, those forms require *more* attention to patterning in order to function in lyric mode—and the same is true for the lyric essay.

In fact, let's demonstrate how this syntactical patterning applies to a few examples. Back in *The Art of Syntax*, Voigt says poetry makes use of "two often-competing rhythmic systems: the rhythm of syntax . . . which poetry shares with well-made prose, and the rhythm of the line." Poets negotiate between these systems, "whether a line will be primarily consonant with the syntax, parsing it, or dissonant, in counterpoint" (Voigt 2009, 24). Voigt contrasts Kunitz's short, parsing lines that break his sentences into coherent syntactic chunks with Lawrence's long, mostly end-stopped lines, and says that while Kunitz micromanages the syntax for us, Lawrence's are macromanagers: "the poet [hurls] large chunks at us, creating a 'torrent' of words he wants us to gulp down whole . . . long, propulsive musical phrasing" (36–7).

We might compare this to the "micromanaging" of syntax in Theresa Cha's *Dictee*, where the short sentences and sentence fragments parse and reshuffle a small handful of words, adding layers of nuance and meaning that persists beyond the attempts of "she" to erase them: "She forgets. She tries to forget. For the moment. For the duration of these moments" (Cha 2001, 113). In contrast, we get a macromanaging "torrent" of words from Hanif Abdurraqib in "On Times I Have Forced Myself to Dance": ". . . & so no one saw my brief moment of rhythm before it unraveled and just like that I was in a pile of discarded shoes & it is safest to say that there was no girlfriend for me that summer or the summer after & . . ." (Abdurraqib 2022, 4). We'll see more of this parsing-versus-torrent when we compare Aburraqib's one-sentence lyric essay torrent with the forceful but more parsed one-sentence piece by Diane Seuss, [I hoisted them, two drug dealers], a little later in this discussion.

In the absence of lines, other strategies are needed to parse or "chunk" the syntax for the reader. This might take the form of punctuation (see my essay "A Dash of Dash" for the various flavors). Otherwise, the writer must use other visual or typographical means to parse the syntax, inserting slash marks or white space (which essentially function as in-text line breaks), and/or use fragments. Inserting slash marks appears to be a technique borrowed from contemporary prose poetry, used instead of lines and/or punctuation, and is seen in this piece by Billy-Ray Belcourt:

> PICTURE THIS: TWO BROTHERS, ONE FINDS IN BOOZE WHAT THE OTHER FINDS IN THE BODIES OF WHITE MEN / REFUSE TO THINK THE CONSEQUENCES OF THESE CRAVINGS AS ANYTHING BUT EQUALLY POISONOUS / I AM NO BETTER THAN HE WHO EATS TOO MUCH OF THE SUNSET / IN FACT ALL I DO IS GNAW AND GNAW AT THE SUN UNTIL MY LIPS ARE SO CRACKED THAT I CAN ONLY SPEAK THE WORLD WRONG /.
>
> (Washuta and Warburton 2019, 103)

Or, in Rajiv Mohabir's "Amazon River Dolphin," from his hybrid memoir *Antiman*:

> // There are river dolphins in the Ganges // There are river dolphins in Guyanese rivers // Your echolocation vibes with both species // How queer for a dolphin to live in a river // Diaspora is a queer country // How can you be at once two species from two places //.
>
> (Mohabir 2021, 156)

The presence of these slash marks in hybrid texts suggests it's a way of functioning between lineated poetry and lyric prose. And as I pointed out in "Mind the Gap," Sheila O'Connor uses white space to embody the silences surrounding her biological grandmother's history in *Evidence of V*, but we also see the white space and fragments sealing off these pregnant incarcerated girls into scraps of history. The fragments are themselves sentence fragments, without active verbs and using passive voice or verbs shunted into participial adjectives to emphasize their lack of agency:

> [. . .
> . . .
> Shhh.   The sound of V is silence.
>
> Girl of sealed history like all those other girls.
> Sealed; therefore buried.

> State documents I now excavate for answers.
> An official file of facts that read like fiction.
>
> V a fiction built of fragments, as girls so often are.]
> (O'Connor 2019, 1)

These brief spaces give the reader a pause in which to make sense of those chunks. The lyric essayist might even, ultimately, resort to lineation to reclaim that "tension of competing systems," as in Lee Ann Roripaugh's haibun "Inquiline," where the short lyric prose suddenly distills to a haiku-moment in which the first two lines parse the image into two separate iterations of draining, making it seem like there's nothing left, no tears, until the second line break/third line completes the thought in a withering rejection:

> like a bird who doesn't even wake while the Madagascan moth slides a plundering tongue under its eyelids, secretly drinking away all the bird's tears.
>
> > This phlebotomized
> > and thief-parched heart has no tears
> > left over for you.
> > (Roripaugh 2014, 91)

I do want to highlight one fascinating point Longenbach makes, though. Longenbach "suggests that we inevitably think about lineation when we read a prose poem" (Longenbach 2008, 94), saying that "The effect of our more typical notion of a prose poem depends on the deletion of lineation from the formal decorum of poetry, and the absence of the line would not be interesting if we did not feel the possibility of its presence" (87–8). I'm trying to decide if I agree and whether this has an application for the lyric essay. I think this comes down to the idea of the contract between writer and reader: by calling a piece of writing a prose poem, the poet is engaging with what the reader expects from a poem—a main feature of which would be lineation—so its absence creates the tension of a "possibility of its presence." Does this same effect occur in the lyric essay? I'm not sure that it does. While up until now, the "lyric" part of lyric essay has suggested a grab bag of effects, the reader still largely expects to see prose, however stylized. Therefore the possibility of the line's presence doesn't exist, unless the writer explicitly suggests that possibility with visual or typographic breaks. It also brings up an interesting way to answer the question, Does it matter what we call a piece of writing? In the case of two writers whose work I've discussed elsewhere—Diane Seuss's [I hoisted them, two drug dealers] and Lee Ann Roripaugh's "Lee Aster"—each published these pieces in books published as poetry, though Roripaugh has since acknowledged she thinks of the language-betrayal pieces as lyric essays (Czerwiec 2020), and [I hoisted them, two drug dealers] was first published in *Brevity* as flash prose. Does calling them poems allow them to evoke that tension of the possibility of the line by working against readers' expectations? Likewise, do Kathy Fish's "Collective Nouns for Humans in the Wild" and Nicole Walker's "Fish," both published as flash prose, subvert that contract with the reader when their prose breaks into lines? These specific examples don't mean all lyric essays create that possibility of the line, but it does suggest there are certain suggestive ways to do it.

Before I turn to examples of how Voigt's and Longenbach's craft discussions about lyric syntax apply to the lyric essay, I want to acknowledge that the craft I'm citing has been talking about the prose poem, which I've been applying to the lyric essay, which begs the question, What is the difference between the prose poem and lyric essay? Again, I would point to what I say at the end of "Strike a Chord," where I note Amy Lowell's concept of the "rate of return": the recurrence of resonances is denser the more we approach "pure poetry"; therefore, we would expect this patterning to be more dense in a prose poem than in a lyric essay, though there's not a definitive demarcation. However, these are strategies that can and should apply to the lyric essay.

For two examples of how lyric essayists compensate for absence of line with increased attention to structure, to patterns of syntax and sound and image, I'm going to look at two lyric essay piece each written as single sentences, which amplify the various strategies employed to trace their process of mind, to convey meaning and make music simultaneously.

I've discussed Diane Seuss's [I hoisted them, two drug dealers] in "Strike a Chord," but to recap, she captures the fierce rage and anger and love of the mother of an addict, attempting to drive out his dealers, and somehow manages to pair the violence of his C-section birth with the threat he's become (Seuss 2021a, 67). While the piece as punctuated is one sentence, all the parsing is accomplished by commas dividing up the text, controlling the flow of this firehose of text. Besides the energy of the driving sentence, energy is also created by the repetition of the subject-verb-object syntactical unit "I __-ed them," where the verb is a violent action of lifting or cutting: "I hoisted them," "I exiled them," "I excised them," "I pulled them." Some of these verbs, "exiled," "excised," and "excommunicated," though they are spaced apart, call across to each other because of the similarity of the words, all beginning with "ex-," and that they're uncommon verbs so they stick out, syntax and sound united, all structures of thinking that assert—to herself and to us—how she's trying to cut off the addict son who was once cut from her body. Sometimes she uses short appositive phrases and commas to pivot the sentence. Seuss does this twice with the phrase "my son," surrounding it with other short comma-ed off phrases: first when getting rid of the dealers in the basement apartment turns her concern to her son, which makes her remember the violence of his birth: ". . . left behind a concrete floor full of dog shit, and he, my son, I gave birth to him in 1985, it was a hard labor in a small town hospital and they had to cut me open, don't knock me out I yelled, after all this I want to be awake when you lift out the kid,. . ." before that lifting image leads to a refrain of the opening "and I hoisted those two dealers"; and second, when after chasing off the dealers makes her briefly recall a memory of her and her sister biking in floodwaters, her thoughts turn back to her son: ". . .riding our bikes through that water which must have been full of shit, my son, he was nowhere to be found, I didn't see him until, what was it. . ." Those short, parsed phrases slow us down somewhat so we can make that pivot without jumping the rails of her train of thought. Seuss often includes asides that explicitly trace her thought process, inserting such phrases as "I guess," "well," "must have been," "what was it," and "is what I'm saying," as well as descriptive associations of "like." At the end, when her wrath has become so godlike she doesn't even need to use her hands, she uses syntax to sum up her point in two parallel anaphoric phrases to slam on the brakes: "don't ask for my touch is what I'm saying, don't ask me to now walk among the people."

The first piece in Hanif Abdurraqib's collection *A Little Devil in America* is likewise a single-sentence lyric essay, "On Times I Have Forced Myself to Dance" (Abdurraqib 2022, 3–4). However, where Seuss uses phrases parsed by commas to steer us through the flow of her rage and the pivots between past and present, Abdurraqib's piece includes no punctuation except for the final period, but uses the ampersand symbol to allow for the accrual of clauses and to make connections between a confluence of events of two summers, an effect which also keeps the piece in motion much like him practicing smooth dance moves and in particular the moonwalk which glides smoothly with no breaks. He also uses the refrain "safe to say," which creates sonic resonance but also demonstrates the author considering the significance of and possible connections or even cause-and-effect between this confluence of events, structures of thinking created by this union of syntax (coordinating clauses) and resonance (refrain). "Safe to say" is often followed by a negating or isolating phrase ("none of the other," "only one," "no") to show the author's isolation:

> Safe to say none of the other Muslim kids on the eastside of Columbus got MTV or BET in their cribs . . . & so it is also safe to say that I was the only one in the Islamic Center on Broad Street who got to stay up and watch the shows . . . & so it is safe to say that I only danced along the slick surface of my basement floor . . . & I do not want a spirit to enter me but I do want a girlfriend . . . & it is absolutely safe to say that with my socks on the marbled tile of the Islamic Center on Broad Street I felt overcome by something we will call holy.
>
> (ellipses mine)

The phrase also sets up the lack of safety at the end—first wryly comical, then brutal—when, while trying to show off the moonwalk for other young people, he slides into the stairwell: ". . . & so no one saw my brief moment of rhythm before it unraveled and just like that I was in a pile of discarded shoes & it is safest to say that there was no girlfriend for me that summer or the summer after & the cable at my house got cut off the year my mother died."

Lyric Structures: Structure versus Form

So far, we've looked at how writers use these structures and shapes of thinking and sound at the level of the sentence. But these structures of thinking also expand beyond the sentence. They build from the sentence outward: the shape of chunks within a sentence, the shape of the sentence, and the shape of paragraphs all create syntactic rhythms, "arrangements of pattern and variation, balance and asymmetry, repetition and surprise" (Voigt 2009, 20). But the structures of thinking, the arrangement of patterns, may be imposed from the top down as well, to pair a particular shape of content to a particular shape or form. In the case of the lyric essay, that structure of thinking is lyric—the form can come from any genre or any source, even non-literary.

This linking of the sentence structure to the larger structure of the overall piece, and its connection to thought, is echoed by Helen Vendler in her "Introduction to *The Art of Shakespeare's Sonnets*" (reprinted in *The Lyric Theory Reader*), when she asserts the key criteria appropriate for judging lyric is, "How well does the structure of this poem mimic the structure of thinking? and How well does the linguistic play of the poem embody that structural mimesis?" (Jackson and Prins 2014, 130). This is why, when we hit on the perfect form for a piece of writing, the piece seems to write itself: because how you've been thinking about the material gets perfectly aligned or reflected in the form—the structures match up.

So what kinds of larger structures and forms (again, not the same thing) are we seeing in the lyric essay, and how do those pair with structures of thinking?

Radiant Lyre, an excellent collection of critical work on lyric poetry, names and explores the history and strategies of the lyric's dominant subgenres—elegy, love poem, ode, pastoral—noting that although we popularly conceive of the lyric as private, the lyric also has a long history of public performance of the personal (Baker 2007). I argue these structures of thinking persist in many of the lyric essays written today and are participating in that public performance of the personal by connecting the "this is what it felt like" to "this is what it meant and why it matters." For instance, consider Brian Doyle's "Leap" as a

9/11 elegy or Claudia Rankine's *Citizen* as elegy and inquest into the deaths of young Black men. The pieces of Aimee Nezhukumatathil's *World of Wonders* and several of the pieces in Ross Gay's *The Book of Delights*, such as "The Jenky," as odes. And, in fact, the lyric essays under ecowriting would qualify either as pastoral—calling attention to an ideal natural world—or as pastoral elegy, literally in the sense of an elegy for the pastoral, in the moment of its disappearing due to the climate crisis. These larger subgenres are structures of thinking and are inscribed in a number of forms: for instance, many of Nezhukumatathil's odes are written as braids, while Gay's often are flash. But the lyric strategies of patterning employed to convey that thinking are what make these lyric essays.

Lyric essays may also take their structure and shape from verse forms drawn from poetry. Because I describe that strategy extensively in my essay "Using Poetic Forms in Nonfiction," I'll just point to it and not belabor it here.

The shapes Jane Alison describes in *Meander, Spiral, Explode* also have been useful for thinking about alternatives to traditional narrative structures. Her book includes the title forms, as well as waves and wavelets (more recurrent than the singular rise/fall of narrative) and cell-like compartmentalized moments that combine to create something larger and hivelike (Alison 2019).

In *Shapes of Native Nonfiction*, editors Theresa Warburton and Elissa Washuta explain how they've ordered their collection based on terms applied to basket weaving: technique (craft essays), coiling (essays that appear seamless, not fragmented, often growing in spirals, and "constructed using transitional gestures"), plaiting (fragmented/segmented essays that "include material from a single source, usually the author's lived experience"), and twining ("essays that bring together material from different sources") (Washuta and Warburton 2019, 17).

In her introduction to the recent collection *A Harp in the Stars: An Anthology of Lyric Essays*, which was also republished in a shorter form online in *Brevity*, editor Randon Billings Noble states, "Despite its resistance to categorization, there are broad forms of the lyric essay that are worth trying to define." She lists these as flash essays ("short, sharp, and clarifying"); segmented essays "divided into segments that might be numbered or titled or simply separated with a space break" and which she notes are also known as fragmented, paratactic, collage, or mosaic essays; braided essays, which are "segmented essays whose sections have a repeating pattern—the way each strand of a braid returns to take its place in the center . . . its meaning is enriched by the other strands you've read through"; and hermit crab essays, which "borrow another [extraliterary] form of writing as their structure the way a hermit crab borrows another's shell" (Noble 2021, xiii–xvi). I agree with Noble that these forms are used extensively in lyric essays, though I respectfully disagree or would ask for a finer distinction: I would call them mostly nonlinear creative nonfiction forms that might be lyric, depending on whether they employ lyric strategies, rather than lyric essay forms outright. Just as the essay might use lyric forms (ode, elegy, sonnet) but turn (or re-turn) them back to their public performance to incorporate the larger "so what?," the lyric might use creative nonfiction forms—especially those that appeal to the lyric's nonlinear sensibilities—to its own purposes. And I get the appeal—in the absence of the line and line break, the lyric essayist looks to other strategies to disrupt linear progression and reincorporate some of that white space and surprise.

How are these forms (which, again, can be drawn from any source), especially the nonlinear creative nonfiction forms, steered to lyric ends? According to Vendler, lyric strategies that mimic/enact the structure of thinking (all of which involve introducing new linguistic strategies) include the following:

- introducing new sets of words
- introducing new stylistic arrangements (syntax, grammar, phonetics)
- change in topic
- change in syntactic structure (say, from parallelism to chiasmus) (Jackson and Prins 2014, 130).

These strategies obviously work with segmented essays and braids (introducing new topics or diction), with essays that make different lateral moves (change in syntactic structure, say from parallelism/

apposition or juxtaposition to chiasmus/opposition), or in essays involving turns (such as my labyrinth essay). But it's important to note that with "sets of words" (which involves language/texture), and "phonetics" and "syntax" or "syntactic structure" (which involve sound both explicitly and implicitly), this attention to language patterning is lyric. Vendler is talking about poems, so she's already assuming a level of resonance in the language. But because we're applying these lyric strategies that signal thinking to our discussion of the lyric essay, I want to make sure to reiterate that these strategies would need to be paired with resonance for the essay to be functioning lyrically.

All of these lyric strategies are ultimately structured by an evolving inner emotional and/or intellectual dynamic. Both the strategies of the mind thinking and how that thinking progresses through sections obviously could be applied to content the lyric essayist puts into the nonlinear creative nonfiction forms Noble names.

In fact, theorist Nigel Krauth suggests these strategies of syntactic chunking, fragments, and nonlinear forms might also mimic the *reader's* structure of thinking. Although his critical essay is titled "Fragmented *Narratives*" (italics mine), he keeps calling such strategies and structures "poetic." Citing Walter Benjamin's theorizing that we think in fragments, Krauth argues, "The brevity and cryptic nature of [such forms] makes it seductive: the reader engages easily, before realising there is more work to do before the promised meaning becomes clear." Such work "sets them on a path toward insight by increasing the bounds of their own thinking" through a "simultaneous engagement of focused and diffuse thinking." He concludes, "When we read, our brains put the bits together subjectively, even when the mode is linear. We . . . are not so hard-wired that we only think linearly as we read" (Krauth 2019).

Bringing Together Structure, Syntax, and Form

Let's look more closely at an example of a lyric essay that traces and engages with both the author's and the reader's "focused and diffuse thinking," demonstrating Vendler's strategies. Jordan K. Thomas's "The Murder of Crows" (Thomas 2015) is a segmented or twined essay, possibly a braid if the threads are loosely categorized as history, culture, and personal. In it, Thomas uses the figure of the crow to trace his thinking about race in America. I chose this example because of its length, since I've been arguing that the lyric essay is not defined by brevity and to show how lyric strategies can be sustained over larger structures. Here, I will express gratitude to Karen Babine for her careful mapping of the various turns this essay makes in her craft piece "On Torque: Turns in Nonfiction," which I'm partially pulling from (Babine 2023). The essay begins with four sections which, while all about crows, shift in notable ways from one to the next: the first is personal observation—"There are no crows in Austin"—and cycles through sentences that reiterate both the driving out of crows here and the author's elsewhere home with crows, in parallel anaphoric structures; the second is an ornithological catalogue of corvids; the third lists mini-narratives of the role of crows in lore; and the fourth uses sonic devices to parallel call-and-response behavior in Africa, worship, and in crows' symbiosis with wolves. The fourth section ends by noting crows cannot fight off eagles, before the piece takes a strong turn in the fifth section to the rise of the term "Jim Crow" and Jim Crow laws, though imagistically the reader is prepared for that leap by the contrast between the eagle (symbol of American ideal) and its attacks on the (Black) crow. From this point, the sections of the essay weave various approaches to Jim Crow—history of Jim Crow laws, etymologies, blackface, and minstrelsy—before returning to crow hunting statutes in Texas and Iowa: "Crows are not protected, not from anyone who considers them a nuisance or threat." Thomas uses repetition at the start of the following section to make the connection—"Jordan Davis was killed for being a nuisance"—before moving into a sequence of segments on lynchings old and recent. He also inserts a segment on the ineffectiveness of scarecrows, adding "Using the bodies of dead crows, however, has proved quite effective. Some farmers would hang them from trees . . . [or] left their bodies to rot in the fields," before shifting to a segment that begins, "Michael Brown was shot dead and left on the ground for four and a half hours." In this stretch of segments, the language describing the lynchings is blunt, juxtaposed and yet not narrative facts, mostly short simple sentences or sentence fragments interspersed with longer, lyrical sentences that push in on a particular image or detail or thought that's struck Thomas, using repetition as he circles a point—"It is known"; "What is there to say about these deaths?"—before making the metaphor explicit: "All our crows are dying." The final segment leaves us with a personal encounter with a crow funeral in a cornfield, which isn't so much an anecdote as a slow zooming in and realization of what's at the gathering's focal point: "a young crow, wings shattered, neck broken, in a crumpled heap," an image spanning American history and geography in the figure of the (Jim) crow. By beginning and ending with personal experiences with crows, this recall also loops the reader back to the start of the essay (an intentional part of this piece's structure) and the double-meaning of the title, and reminds us of more threatening implications of the opening sentence "There are no crows in Austin."

To loop back to the start of my own essay here, to end with repetition, I reiterate what Voigt says about how in lyric writing, with its music, syntax, and structure, "pattern supplants suspense." Thomas's move from crows to Jim Crow might initially surprise us, but it does not create suspense before this reveal, and afterwards, the patterning *is* the argument: Thomas reveals the pattern of behaviors of and against black crows and Black folks. This piece demonstrates how the structures and strategies discussed by Voigt, Vendler, and others can be used to build the lyric essay, creating both syntactic (in meaning and music) and imagistic parallels from sentence to sentence and across sections to show a mind making connections (and, as Krauth suggests, inviting us to make connections ourselves) in writing simultaneously expansive and compressed.

Thinking Cap

On Structures: *Lyric*

Today, my thinking cap is synaptic, is syntactic—a nest of electrodes tracing the firings of my brain—chunks or torrents of words and rhythms, conveying meaning by sound—hard-wired deep structures of theme and its variations creating a fugue state—

My thinking caps take different shapes, but my throat below it keeps vibrating like the strings of a lyre. The shape shapes the song; the song sings the shape into being. They sing and think toward each other. You might call it *scoring* in that there's a soundtrack, in that there's carved marks left on the shape, lyrically inscribed, the way a bone or shell might be notched, to tally, to keep score.

Today my thinking cap is shaped like a **shell**.
See also:
fit to (v.), to which I'm fit (v.), fit as a fiddle (adj., idiomatic), fiddler (n.), hermit crab (n. or adj.)

Today's a hymn of praise! O flamboyant piece of millinery meant for churchgoing! O glory laud and honor! O raise the palms, to psalm, to raise the simple to applause! O tomato plant and corpse flower! O color blue!

My thinking cap is fractal, each crotch: a branch branching, a bough bowing: beneath the weight of freighted limbs untrimmed, both outward and down the trunk sprout sprouts: shoots and rootlings. Or, a creek to stream streaming, tribes of riven tributaries become river, become riverine, flexing its delta.

I must wear my cap with a difference. Jaunty angle; rakish tilt. Today's cap has many brims>Middle English "bank of a body of water," full to the brim. Fragments I have shored. Its music modulates between modes—which way am I facing?—looking way over yonder in a minor key, switching structures and topics, creating friction in the diction. Harsh bells jangled out of tune. Well, how did I get here?

Today my thinking cap is of three minds, like a braid in which there are three blackbirds.
One is a moment, manipulated, dilated, counting always *One*.
One is once upon a time, mythic, folkloric. Will my tale end well? Perhaps, though not as you might expect.
One's once is etymological, once an ounce, for which I shall weigh my words accordingly.
The first will occur, circling its lyric moment like a dog around a treed fox, its scent on the current, recurring.
The second also recurs, a cur. Is it the black dog of omen curling its lip? Or my witchy mistress's lap dog with eyes big as mill wheels?
The third occurrence informs us cur is both growl and house, guard dog who will protect our plaiting.
The three weave like a trio of spinners, howl in chorus, ordain a hum, a chord, a pleasing counterpoint of diction, syntax, and image the writer's mind may multiply.

Today my thinking cap is a beanie, spinning on its axis, a centrifuge sending us to the outer limits like the flying saucer ride at the state fair, or swirling us inexorably inward, spiraled to singularity.

Today   fragmentary   fascinator   of fishnet scrimmed   lots of spaces   little silences   made visible   a contemplation   a completion via reader

Today my thinking cap is elegiac. Pansies for thoughts. Pleurant's veil, a wail in word form, marking the moment or event or person even as it passes. *Why is he gone? How could this happen? Where were you? How should we bear witness?*
How will we go on?

Useful Distinctions, or, Why the Lyric Essay Is a Function, Not a Form

I claim in "Structures of Thinking" that the "lyric" part of "lyric essay" is a structure of thinking, and that the lyric essay can use forms from many different genres, subgenres, and sources. But I want to make a clear and explicit case for why we shouldn't call the lyric essay a form or define it by the forms it may use.

But really, what does it matter? Are there any consequences? What's at stake if we mislabel something a lyric essay?

I don't think this is mere marking of territory. Yes, it's annoying to be the weird miscellaneous category. And as Rose Metal Press editors Abigail Beckel and Kathleen Rooney have lamented, "Sometimes we get submissions from people who seem to think that 'hybrid genre' means 'chaotic mess' or 'anything goes' or 'clean out your drafts folders'" (Beckel and Rooney 2013), descriptors especially applied to the lyric essay. That's why having a shared language to discuss these distinctions matters. It's articulating the *what it's doing on the page*, and not its classification, that takes this from a beef, a staking (steaking?) of territory, instead toward building forward, beefing up an ongoing conversation to help us understand creative nonfiction in its many varieties. If we can create a better, more concrete understanding of what we mean when we say *lyric*, and thereby connect that to an entire preexisting vocabulary of poetic craft so we don't have to reinvent the wheel, then we can notice and point to specific qualities or strategies in lyric essays to note how authors use them to create specific effects. Writers and teachers can also use those lyric qualities or strategies to teach or to revise toward making creative nonfiction more lyric, if that is the intent. But, again, this conversation must arise from describing what the writing is doing on the page.

If—as people who write about, think about, and teach creative nonfiction and perhaps lyric essays—we don't fully theorize what we mean by the "lyric" in lyric essay, then what?

The addition of more anthologies including or comprised of lyric essays to the literary landscape, which are creating and adding to and opening up this ongoing conversation in new and exciting and useful ways, is helping us as we refine these terms. As I noted in "Structures of Thinking," Randon Billings Noble offers her contribution to this nascent discussion in *A Harp in the Stars: An Anthology of Lyric Essays*. In her introduction (Noble 2021, a reprinted version appears in *Brevity*'s blog), she states, "Despite its resistance to categorization, there are broad forms of the lyric essay that are worth trying to define" (xiii). She lists these as flash essays ("short, sharp, and clarifying"); segmented essays "divided into segments that might be numbered or titled or simply separated with a space break" and which she notes are also known as fragmented, paratactic, collage, or mosaic essays; braided essays, which are "segmented essays whose sections have a repeating pattern—the way each strand of a braid returns to take its place in the center. Each time a particular strand returns, its meaning is enriched by the other strands you've read through"; and hermit crab essays, which "borrow another [extraliterary] form of writing as their structure the way a hermit crab borrows another's shell" (xiii–xvi). I'm not interested in trying to rigidly classify what a structure or form is, but rather describe what it's doing and how it's functioning on the page. So a piece might be using a nonlinear nonfiction form or a hermit crab form or, going back to my "Four Temperaments" essay, might be working in more than one mode. But what makes it function lyrically is how lyric strategies of thinking and resonance are deployed to convey an experience.

I agree these forms are used extensively in lyric essays. However, I want to advance this conversation by making the following distinction. They are not "forms of the lyric essay"; I would call them mostly nonlinear creative nonfiction forms that *might* be lyric, depending on whether they employ lyric strategies. Because of course not all nonfiction is linear. But definitions like Noble's seem to argue essays are lyric simply because they are short, nonlinear, and are in one of these forms, yet Cheryl Strayed's *Wild* is a narrative memoir that braids memories of her mother, her grief after her mother's death, details about the Pacific Crest Trail, and the story of Strayed's momentous hike—and it is not lyric. Chris Arthur is fond of the segmented form; Michele Morano's well-known "In the Subjunctive Mood" is also segmented, and neither are lyric. Just as a ten-page Montaignian essay might use lyric forms (ode, elegy, sonnet) but turn (or re-turn) them back to their public performance to incorporate the larger rhetorical "so what?," the lyric might use creative nonfiction forms—especially those that appeal to the lyric's nonlinear sensibilities—to its own purposes, using patterning to explore, impose, or reveal patterns and therefore connections. "Lyric," then, is a function, and when applied as an adjective to lyric essays, it means something specific.

My argument is based on poet and critic Ellen Bryant Voigt's distinction. In the title essay from her craft book *The Flexible Lyric*, she argues *structure* (the thinking mind and the perceived effects of the texture) + *form* (the particular patterned shape of the piece) = *function* (Voigt 1999, 124–31). Let me restate that because it's important: her argument is for a definition of lyric based on *function*, of which form is only a part. This is why Voigt can assert literature might be in the same form and/or subgenre—say, an Elizabethan love sonnet—and yet have different functions: Shakespeare's "Dark Lady" sonnets have a lyric function, yet the sonnet comprising the first spoken dialogue between Romeo and Juliet has a dramatic function. Therefore, she contends, "the important differences lie in the distinct functions to which such materials are put" (149). She's making an argument for lyric not merely as songlike but as a specific function of a specific way of thinking/speaking that has specific strategies: defined not by form but by *what it's doing on the page*.

We're already using forms for our own functions. I point to my own and Noble's and many others' citation of Jane Alison's *Meander, Spiral, Explode* when discussing forms and shapes and patterns in writing. Despite her subtitle, "Design and Pattern in Narrative," non-narrative and lyric essayists (myself included) have been positively gleeful about appropriating the shapes she describes. And that's great, because it demonstrates how they can be put to a different function—like the lyric essay—even though Alison conceived of them as narrative and applies them to analyses of fiction and narrative nonfiction.

Shapes of Native Nonfiction, edited by Elissa Washuta and Theresa Warburton, is a good example of what happens when we start to talk about the function of a piece of nonfiction, rather than its form: its essays are classified by participial adjectives that describe what an essay is *doing* on the page—coiling, plaiting, twining (Washuta and Warburton 2019). If/when we reorient the language and the approach, we gain more of a focus on craft choices: Why *this* form with *this* content? How is it shaping and building how we experience the writing? What genre strategies are being deployed and to what end?

Here, I wish to return to Judith Kitchen's assertion:

> The term [lyric essay] had been minted (brilliantly, it seems to me) by Deborah Tall, then almost immediately undermined. Not all essays are lyric. Repeat. Not all essays are lyric. Not even all short essays are lyric. Some are merely short. Or plainly truncated. Or purely meditative. Or simply speculative. Or. Or. Or. But not lyric. Because, to be lyric, there must be a lyre.
>
> (Kitchen 2007, 47)

As a result of focusing on defining lyric essays by form rather than function, I feel there are essays in *A Harp in the Stars* that are *not* functioning as lyric essays. In Noble's introduction, she explains, "I came to define a lyric essay as a piece of writing with a visible / stand-out / unusual structure [here, Noble seems to be using "structure" as synonymous with "form"] that explores / forecasts / gestures to an idea in an unexpected way" (Noble 2021, xiii), before going on to list and describe "the broad forms of the lyric essay." But, as I asked before, what's at stake if we call pieces lyric essays when they're not?

I thought it might be helpful for me to compare a few essays in *A Harp in the Stars* that share the same form in order to illustrate the difference between lyric essay as form versus function and to argue for what can be gained if we discuss them instead in terms of function.

Both Susanna Donato's "Classified" and Michael Dowdy's "Elementary Primer" are labeled "hermit crab essays" (though Donato's is also labeled "segmented"). I've selected these two because both employ an alphabetical organization: Donato's according to definition and Dowdy's as an abecedarian. Both Donato and Dowdy make use of the possibilities of a similar hermit crab form, but to different ends and therefore functions—Donato to add depth to her narrative and Dowdy to lyrically emphasize the role of repetition and patterning in his fears for his daughter.

Donato's essay is a story about a summer relationship started through a classified ad. Donato is at a transitional point in her life in many ways—in a waning friendship and looking for another, trying to decide whether she must or should drop out of her Ivy League college, and who she is and wants to become: "I was learning to decide what I wanted. How" (66). The young man (though several years older, mid-twenties) whom she meets, "Weird Brian," is a drifting, somewhat pretentious goth, though because Donato currently also feels driftless, unattached, and like an outsider at school, he appeals to her: "Each quirk I tolerated—his florid handwriting, his cigarette holder—restored me to my original self. . . . His affectations abashed me" (63). The essay is organized according to the definitions for "Classified," where each segment relates to a different definition, progressing a, b, c, d. While versions of the word "classified" recur throughout this piece, acting as a motif as she tries to define him, their relationship, and herself, the topic, language/diction, and syntax remain the same throughout (the latter mostly subject-verb-object constructions), and the text itself does not seem to be motivated by music or sound effects. Thus, we have the opportunity to talk about the function of something that differs from a lyric strategy, about how this form can be put to other uses.

The piece's inner thought processes, including questions as she tries to define identity, demonstrate character development. If the piece's function were lyric, however, I might expect to see it jump around more in time to see how this relationship rippled outward, or engage in "perhapsing" by imagining alternate scenes or outcomes or people they might have become (Knopp 2009), or pushing into the language of "classified" more. Most tellingly, in a lyric essay, in which the function of the piece is lyric, the logical organization of its structure—how the sections relate to each other—would be apposition or opposition or a change in style or rhetoric; here, it is largely chronological, if arranged in episodes. As a result, though it does allow for meditative moments of authorial reflection, this piece is a story, so its function is narrative, not lyric. This form allows the author to frame the story, so we get not only the premise of the classified ad but also the various ways they classify each other, which does add depth. It's a great piece and is a good example of using a hermit crab form to shape its narrative.

In contrast, Michael Dowdy's "Elementary Primer," an abecedarian addressed to his daughter on entering first grade, is a meditation on violence—specifically, gun violence—in America. This piece is explicitly lyric in its strategy. Dowdy's patterning reveals the stakes, establishing a pattern he's terrified his child will fall into. The first section links school, violence, and death across the map of America, and the words of poets addressing these themes, motifs that will continue to resonate throughout the essay: "**A**, dear daughter, when later this month you begin first grade, remember your letters and numbers, a delight or two, the words of others, the pain of mothers and brothers, all seared onto the pallbearer's atlas of your country like 10,000 crossroads" (99). That map conceit makes the abecedarian more than a mere list of mass shooting sites—Blacksburg, Columbine, Charleston, Dayton, etc.—but ties them together as a web of "crossroads," an "atlas" of deaths. Each section logically builds by accrual, by apposition, and in fact, each section often consists of appositive, anaphoric phrases beginning "where": "**Blacksburg**, where I was born and lived for 24 years, where your beloved grandparents remain, where a college student . . . murdered 32" (99). The sections combine personal, individual details about the daughter's family and about the victims of the shootings that occurred in those places, contrasted in texture with the Arabic numerals of the years, highways, and death counts, parallels that demonstrate Dowdy's sickening fears these entwined histories will converge.

Several of the sections explicitly include lyric language, quoting lines from poets Nikky Finney, Adrian C. Louis, and Juan Felipe Herrera, among others, as well as Weldon Kees's "Travels in North America." Dowdy's own language compresses together images and events to further complicate and reckon with America's history of violence: the shooter at Virginia Tech had been a student of "Nikki Giovanni, the poet who penned a ferocious poem after the assassination of MLK 39 years earlier, the poet who knew a rage when she saw it—murdered 32, including your Aunt R's best friend, a dancer, this 5 years before you were born on a September 11, in New York City" (99). He even acknowledges his own cultural complicity in violence that begets violence—"Gabby Giffords survived a white gunman's bullets, on lands stolen by men like these murderer-men, men who look like your father"—and his own horror he projects onto her—"X, the unknown variable, the next crossroads to be branded on the map, the target I hallucinate on your back"—before finding some solace in Z, which "doesn't appear once on the Wikipedia page 'Mass shootings in the United States,'" creating a space of hope for A and her future (103). All of these demonstrate a mind arguing with itself, using repetition and parallel syntax to mean multiple things simultaneously. Collectively, these lyric strategies point to a lyric function and therefore a lyric essay.

Likewise, we can compare two pieces labeled in the anthology as lyric essays in the flash form: Sandra Beasley's "Depends on Who You Ask" and Casandra López's "Fragment: Strength." Rashomon-like, Beasley's flash in two paragraphs on two separate pages presents a brief narrative about a woman's pit stop at a small-town market/hardware store. The first perspective—the first-person "I" of the woman—describes needing to wake up while driving long distance, so stopping and wandering around the mart, feeling obligated to buy something then, after using the bathroom, feeling obligated to buy something else (165). The second perspective—the first-person plural "we" of the cashiers—casts those actions in a more suggestive, ominous light, using the diction of someone reporting a statement for an official record: "*She walked into our market and paced the aisles for an hour. She filled a basket with groceries, then returned them all to the shelves. Instead she bought a bottle of gin, came back for a pack of razor blades, and drove away. We never saw her again*" (166). The few lyrical moments of descriptive imagery—"my head kept nodding toward the steering wheel. The car rumbled along a strip marking the edge of the lane"—are designed to create a particular tone for the first narrator; the telling of the brief story and the projected imagining of the cashiers' perspective are narrative, even fictive. The meaning the author is making lies in the gap between the two interpretive versions of the brief story. In doing so, it highlights its narrative function and how the exact same set of events may tell different stories.

López's "Fragment: Strength" uses the central metaphor of boundaries and how they are breached to explore issues of power and powerlessness: boundaries of flesh, of consent, of persona, of land, of various kinds of autonomy. To say it functions lyrically refers not only to resonances in densely patterned language but also to patterns of thought represented by syntax and other larger structures. It is these strategies, and not just the form, that determine whether a piece is functioning as lyric, which is what makes López's piece a lyric essay—not pretty language.

As a child, she has a lisp and struggles with her mouth and her body: "What right to have to gaze upon myself, to let my fat spill out without boundaries" (132); her family history, both immediate and ancestral, is rife with violations collapsed by the parallel anaphora of "Once":

> Once upon a time I was older and police were raiding my family home. They wanted to open so much. . . . Once I abandoned Brother running into the night to survive Bullet. . . . Once upon a time I was not born, but my ancestors believed I would live. They held that belief in their breath even when the Spanish came and took and took and then the Americans came and took and took and then the Mormons.
>
> (132–3)

As an adult in a BDSM relationship, these boundaries resonate in new, more complicated ways: "I order my lover to his knees and I grow so tall the roof can't contain me . . . right here I'm rooted strong. . . . My lover wants me to break him, and I want to never again be broken" (133). The way she thinks through the multiple ways boundaries may be crossed or broken, the variety of the syntactical structures and music (parallelism of anaphora and colonizers taking, the reversal of the last line, the varying sentence lengths) all indicate an essay constructed with intentional lyric strategies.

I'm not suggesting that this mislabeling is confined to this anthology. It's no coincidence that Judith Kitchen's assertion of "there must be a lyre" is made not long after D'Agata published *The Next American Essay* (D'Agata 2003), one of the only other anthologies devoted to the lyric essay and which also contains pieces that don't function lyrically. (I'm only noting these two because D'Agata's *We Might As Well Call It a Lyric Essay* (2014), a reprint of pieces from the *Seneca Review* special issue, is essentially an extension of *The Next American Essay* and includes most of the same authors; as of this writing, the new anthology *The Lyric Essay as Resistance* (2023), edited by Zoë Bossiere and Erica Trabold, has not yet been released). John McPhee's "The Search for Marvin Gardens" braids facts and history about the game Monopoly with personal details, but the primary driver is narrative, not lyric resonance, as we read on to discover whether he will find the elusive location of Marvin Gardens. Susan Griffin's *Red Shoes* is also a braided essay, braiding an argument in assay mode about the dismissal of women's writing, which tends to braid in women's personal experience, braided together with her own personal essay about her relationship with her grandmother who purchased a pair of red shoes for Griffin. In Griffin's essay, the braid form is part of her argument, but that argument is not framed lyrically. On the other hand, Mary Ruefle's flash piece "Monument" is an example of work of hers that she's described as "figments of my imagination" or "fictional essays" (Ruefle 2009). "Monument" is full of lyric resonance and therefore functions lyrically—but because of its fictive, fable-like quality, not based in nonfiction or signaling a "perhapsing" or imagined event based on nonfiction, it more accurately would be labeled a prose poem, which allows for supreme fictions, rather than a lyric essay which allows only "lyre, not liar."

When we identify lyric essays by form instead of by function, we preemptively shut down the opportunity to discuss how those same forms can be put to different uses in different modes. Lyric essayists don't own the braid or flash forms, even if they're favorites. We also lose the opportunity to thoughtfully articulate in what ways our work is truly hybrid—what strategies from different genres are being combined, but also to what purpose or function. If we judge something incorrectly labeled a lyric essay, we may unfairly critique it, especially where "lyric" gets coded as "good" or "pretty language," where if it's not "lyric" then it's somehow lesser-than. And, ultimately, we fail to define what we mean by the "lyric" of lyric essay, which means we don't move the discourse forward in ways it needs to be moved and developed.

I acknowledge my opinion isn't definitive and may not be the best one. We're still early in the process of defining the lyric essay—which is an exciting moment!—but that process is and should continue to be a conversation.

Epilogue: Recital

Like writing in books, it took me a while to be comfortable with marking up my music. But, like books, once I did, I annotated *everything*.

I originally was a music performance major, and looking back at my flute music, those scores of notes have scores of notes to myself—not only breath marks, those little commas above the melody to punctuate my phrasing, but also stage directions (it was, after all, a performance major) such as "dramatic pause," "with emphasis," "no vibrato."

So this is a call for lyric essayists to mark up your work before you perform it aloud. I came to writing lyric nonfiction by way of poetry and, like poetry, both rely heavily on the sonic resonance of language. Because of this, you should be reading your work aloud already, as you're composing and revising, to maximize and refine those effects. But in the happy event you're invited to give a reading of your work, you should prepare for it like the performance it is. In fact, it used to be standard practice to hire an actor to give readings of literary works, because authors weren't considered qualified. But after performances by poets like Edna St. Vincent Millay or Robert Frost in the early twentieth century, audiences came to appreciate and expect the authenticity of the authorial reading. Performance should be part of your practice. Marking up your work can help.

Remember, readers can read your piece for themselves anytime—the purpose of a performance is to entertain, to give an experience of the work the audience couldn't get otherwise. Some advice is standard: choose your work ahead of time, and time it out so you're well within your limit; if it's difficult to read from your book, hold it up to advertise it to the audience and then read from a printed-out copy in larger type. Don't eat a big meal beforehand; have water handy to sip. Watch videos of poets and lyric essayists reading to get a sense of what you like or dislike in a performance, what works, what you want to emulate or avoid—Ross Gay, Nicole Walker, Lee Ann Roripaugh, Diane Seuss, Brian Doyle, and Aimee Nezhukumatathil are all fantastic performers of their work for different reasons, and videos of them are available online.

But marking up your reading copies is important preparation for a performance. Here are some of my notes, many cribbed from music and poetry practice, but use whatever system works for you:

- Note on the first page the time it takes to read a piece. This can also be helpful for assembling a playlist for performances of different lengths. If you might be excerpting a longer piece, note the length of time it takes to read various passages in the margin, as well as any jumps you might make.

- Outline any necessary introductory comments, as well as how long it takes to deliver them. These could include any context or background the audience needs to know, though hopefully the piece explains most of that itself. I like to give a heads-up on any structural or formal features they can listen for.

- Know your pieces well enough so you will be able to look up and at your audience while reading. You can even doodle a small eye (my doodle has lashes!) at those points.

- Where should you breathe? I indicate this with breath marks from music, like hovering commas or apostrophes ('), above the space between the words where I need to catch my breath. If a passage should be read in a rush without pausing, I indicate this as well, writing "quickly, breathlessly" in the margin.

- Are there words that need extra emphasis for inflection or meaning? I either underline them or add a stress mark above them, the way accented syllables are noted in dictionary pronunciations (´).

- How are you pacing your piece? Just as music includes directions like *con brio* or *rallentando*, make notes for where you want to speed up or slow down your reading to match the content or effect. Keep in mind that if reading quickly, your audience still needs to be able to understand you.

- Should your voice be louder or softer? Like pace, volume can also match content or be used for effect to catch the attention. I usually mark these *f* for *forte* or *p* for *piano*. Again, keep in mind that a little loudness goes a long way, and no audience wants to be shouted at; conversely, while it's nice to have an audience leaning forward in their seats, they still need to be able to hear you.

- Respect the white space in your piece. Silences—rests—are part of music. You can even mark how many beats it should last. If you want to pause longer than a breath mid- or between sentences, mark it—I use a caesura (//). For a brief pause, longer than a breath but shorter than a caesura, I use a linebreak slash (/). And allow for silence at the end of your piece, for the audience to absorb what you just read to them.

And some special cases:

- Are there words, especially in a foreign language, that might be difficult to pronounce? Write phonetic pronunciations over them. When I realized I would be reading the first time from my haibun sequence on perfume, which includes a lot of perfume names, I panicked. I called one of my perfume friends who speaks exquisite French and recorded her saying the names. Learn and practice those pronunciations!

- A reading is largely a sonic, not a visual, performance, and you don't want to mime wildly like a hack actor. But if you think incorporating a specific move or gesture will be effective, note it. (I cock my head when asking a specific question in a couple of different essays.) Poetry Out Loud is a recitation contest sponsored by the NEA, a bit like a very involved bee. In their guidelines for preparation, they emphasize how performers might embody a piece: judges evaluate if recitation "reflects internalization" of a piece: any gestures, expressions, and movements should feel "appropriate" and "essential" to conveying a piece's meaning.

- And yet part of the performance is persona—a mix of the sonic and visual—who are you when you read? Charisma is a difficult quality to generate, but you should consider the self-as-performer you become. Does your reading persona change depending on what work you're reading from, or even change between pieces? Think this out in advance and note that persona at the top of the piece as a reminder. When I read my perfume pieces, I'm a bit flirty, since perfume is about desire; when I read my fracking sequence, my persona is serious, but changes slightly between segments, from more angry and aggressive in the violent parts, to earnest and urgent, to quiet and grave.

- Are there asides you want to make to your audience that need to be made in the middle of the reading, rather than during opening remarks? Mark those. For instance, when reading "Success in Circuit," where I use wordplay between "clew" and "clue," I pause to quickly spell which one I mean when necessary ("clew: c-l-e-w"). But keep asides brief! You don't want to take the audience out of the experience of the piece to go off on a long tangent.

- If your piece is hybrid or experimental, it may incorporate (typo)graphic or visual elements. Figure out ahead of time if there's a way to translate the visual elements into your performance. You might describe or explain them in your opening remarks, or read the different elements in different styles, or even project images of the piece as you read. Find a way to do this that will complement, rather than distract from, your performance.

Finally, approach the performance itself like a musician. Know as much about the performance space as possible: the lighting, acoustics, and ambient noise; the layout of the space and where you'll be located relative to your audience. Warm up and get your instrument in tune, whatever that means to you (yoga breathing, voice exercises, passage run-throughs).

And, after taking your place and thanking the host and audience, let the silence build, for a moment, before you begin.

REFERENCES

Abdurraqib, Hanif. 2022. *A Little Devil in America*. New York: Random House.
Ackerman, Diane. 1990. "Smell." In *A Natural History of the Senses*, 3–63. New York: Vintage.
Ali, Agha Shahid. 1992. "Ghazal: The Charms of a Considered Disunity." In *The Practice of Poetry*, edited by Robin Behn and Chase Twichell, 187–90. New York: HarperPerennial.
Ali, Agha Shahid. 2002. "Ghazal: To Be Teased into DisUnity" In *An Exaltation of Forms*, edited by Annie Finch and Kathrine Varnes, 210–16. Ann Arbor: University of Michigan Press.
Alison, Jane. 2019. *Meander, Spiral, Explode: Design and Pattern in Narrative*. New York: Catapult.
Alvarado, Beth. 2021. "Essays All: However We Decide to Collect Them." *River Teeth*, May 4. https://www.riverteethjournal.com/blog/2021/05/04/essays-all-however-we-decide-to-collect-them?fbclid=IwAR2C5vCs1lyhNQ0yHa9SNZm0ecPxXvMazQCBpFQkB9zJXdWYfZzJXdWYfZW (accessed May 4, 2021).
Alvarez, María Isabel. 2016. "Strawberry Girl: A Prose Sestina." *Gulf Coast: A Journal of Literature and Fine Arts* (Summer). https://gulfcoastmag.org/online/summer-2016/strawberry-girl/ (accessed August 9, 2018).
Babine, Karen. 2020. "A Taxonomy of Nonfiction; Or the Pleasures of Precision." *Literary Hub*, August 3. https://lithub.com/a-taxonomy-of-nonfiction-or-the-pleasures-of-precision/ (accessed August 3, 2020).
Babine, Karen. 2023. "On Torque: Turns in Nonfiction." *AWP Chronicle* (September 2023).
Baker, David. 2007. *Radiant Lyre: Essays on Lyric Poetry*, edited by David Baker and Ann Townsend. Saint Paul: Graywolf Press.
Ballenger, Bruce. 2018. "A Narrative Logic of the Personal Essay." *The Writer's Chronicle* 5 (March): 22–9.
Bascom, Tim. 2013. "Picturing the Personal Essay." *Creative Nonfiction* 49 (Summer). Archived at https://creativenonfiction.org/writing/picturing-the-personal-essay-a-visual-guide/.

Beasley, Sandra. 2014. "On Lyric Essays." At *Chicks Dig Poetry* (author's blog), posted March 26. http://sbeasley.blogspot.com/2014/03/on-lyric-essays.html (accessed June 8, 2020).

Beaulieu, Denyse. 2012. *The Perfume Lover: A Personal History of Scent*. New York: St. Martin's Press.

Beckel, Abigail and Kathleen Rooney. 2013. "Interview with Rose Metal Press." *Flash Fiction Chronicles*, May. https://everydayfiction.com/flashfictionblog/ (accessed September 9, 2022).

Biondolillo, Chelsea. 2019. *The Skinned Bird*. Hamilton, NY: Kernpunkt Press.

Biss, Eula. 2008. "Time and Distance Overcome." *The Iowa Review* 38.1 (Spring): 83–9.

Biss, Eula. 2020. "Reading and Conversation with Maggie Nelson." Filmed September 10, 2020, at Women & Children First Bookstore. YouTube video, 59:20. https://www.youtube.com/watch?v=ltK_XDtTBAA (accessed September 23, 2020).

Bonnaffons, Amy. 2016. "Bodies of Text: On the Lyric Essay." *The Essay Review*. http://theessayreview.org/bodies-of-text-on-the-lyric-essay/ (accessed July 27, 2021).

Boully, Jenny. 2002. *The Body: An Essay*. Buffalo, NY: Essay Press.

Burd, Jennifer. 2015. "White Space as Metaphoric Frame." *Poets' Quarterly*, August. http://www.poetsquarterly.com/2015/08/white-space-as-metaphoric-frame.html (accessed March 7, 2022).

Cage, John. 1959. "Lecture on Nothing." *Incontri Musicali*, August. Archived at https://seansturm.files.wordpress.com/2012/09/john-cage-lecture-on-nothing.pdf (accessed March 7, 2022).

Carson, Anne. 2010. *Nox*. New York: New Directions.

Cha, Sam. 2019. "Unbearable Splendor: Against 'Hybrid' Genre; Against Genre." *Assay: A Journal of Nonfiction Studies* 5.2 (Spring). https://www.assayjournal.com/sam-cha-8203unbearable-splendor-against-hybrid-genre-against-genre-52.html (accessed March 7, 2022).

Cha, Theresa Hak Kyung. 2001. *Dictee*. Berkeley: University of California Press.

Coles, Katharine. 2019. "If a Body." *Assay: A Journal of Nonfiction Studies* 5.2 (Spring). https://www.assayjournal.com/katharine-coles-8203if-a-body-52.html (accessed May 20, 2019).

Cortese, Claudia. 2013. "The Red Essay." *Mid-American Review* 34.1 (Spring): 25–6.

Czerwiec, Heidi. 2015. "The Poessaytics of Form." Panel at NonfictioNOW 2015. Summarized at *Assay Blog*. https://assayjournal.wordpress.com/2015/10/31/assaynfn15-the-poessaytics-of-form/ (accessed May 20, 2021).

Czerwiec, Heidi. 2018. "The Essay as Unstrung Lyre: Prosody in Nonfiction Forms." Panel at NonfictioNOW 2018. Summarized at

Assay Blog. https://assayjournal.wordpress.com/2018/11/05/nfn18-the-essay-as-unstrung-lyre/ (accessed May 20, 2021).

Czerwiec, Heidi. 2019. *Fluid States*. Warrensburg, MO: Pleiades Press.

Czerwiec, Heidi. 2020. "The Assay Interview Project: Lee Ann Roripaugh." *Assay: A Journal of Nonfiction Studies*, January 4. https://www.assayjournal.com/lee-ann-roripaugh.html.

D'Agata, John. 2003. *The Next American Essay*, edited by John D'Agata. Minneapolis: Graywolf Press.

Dennis, Carl. 2008. "The Temporal Lyric." In *Poet's Work, Poet's Play: Essays on the Practice and the Art*, edited by Daniel Tobin and Pimone Triplett, 236–49. Ann Arbor: University of Michigan Press.

Dillard, Annie. 1977. *Holy the Firm*. New York: Harper & Row.

Doyle, Brian. 2003. *Leaping: Revelations and Epiphanies*. Chicago: Loyola Press.

Doyle, Brian. 2019. *One Long River of Sound*. New York: Little, Brown and Co.

Dungy, Camille T. 2014. "Tell It Slant." *Poetry Foundation Blog*, June 14. https://www.poetryfoundation.org/articles/70128/tell-it-slant (accessed July 27, 2021).

Eleftheriou, Joanna. 2016. "Is Genre Ever New? Theorizing the Lyric Essay in Its Historical Context." *Assay: A Journal of Nonfiction Studies* 4.1 (Spring). https://www.assayjournal.com/joanna-eleftheriou-is-genre-ever-new-theorizing-the-lyric-essay-in-its-historical-context.html (accessed July 27, 2021).

Fajardo, Anika. 2014. "What Didn't Happen." *Redux: A Literary Journal* 128 (May). http://www.reduxlitjournal.com/2014/05/128-what-didnt-happen-by-anika-fajardo.html (accessed April 21, 2021).

Fish, Kathy. 2017. "Collective Nouns for Humans in the Wild." *Jellyfish Review*, October 13. https://jellyfishreview.wordpress.com/2017/10/13/collective-nouns-for-humans-in-the-wild-by-kathy-fish/ (accessed December 13, 2021).

Fish, Kathy. 2021. "Fractured/Fragmented/Mosaic Flash." *The Art of Flash Fiction Online Newsletter*, June. https://artofflashfiction.substack.com/p/fractured-fragmented-mosaic-flash (accessed June 15, 2021).

Fussell, Paul. 1965. *Poetic Meter and Poetic Form*. New York: Random House.

Glück, Louise. 1994. "Disruption, Hesitation, Silence." In *Proofs and Theories: Essays on Poetry*, 73–85. New York: Ecco Press.

Graham, Jorie. 1984. "Some Notes on Silence" In *19 New American Poets of the Golden Gate*, edited by Philip Dow, 409. New York: Harcourt Brace Jovanovich.

Gross, Harvey and Robert McDowell. 1996. *Sound and Form in Modern Poetry*, 2nd ed. Ann Arbor: University of Michigan Press.

G'Schwind, Stephanie. 2013. "An Artful Placement of Needle Against Album." *Essay Daily*, November 6. http://www.essaydaily.org/2013/11/stephanie-gschwind-artful-placement-of.html (accessed December 10, 2013).

Harad, Alyssa. 2012. *Coming to My Senses: A Story of Perfume, Pleasure, and an Unlikely Bride*. New York: Penguin.

Herman, Barbara. 2013. *Scent & Subversion*. Guilford, CT: Lyons Press.

Hirshfield, Jane. 1997. "Poetry and the Mind of Indirection." In *Nine Gates: Entering the Mind of Poetry*, 107–26. New York: HarperCollins.

Hollander, John. 1988. *Melodious Guile: Fictive Pattern in Poetic Language*. New Haven, CT: Yale University Press.

Huber, Sonya. 2017. "What Pain Wants." In *Pain Woman Takes Your Keys*, 3–6. Lincoln: University of Nebraska Press.

Jackson, Virginia and Yopie Prins, eds. 2014. *The Lyric Theory Reader: A Critical Anthology*. Baltimore: Johns Hopkins University Press.

Jones, Mary Paumier and Judith Kitchen, eds. 1996. *In Short: A Collection of Brief Creative Nonfiction*. New York: Norton.

Kinzie, Mary. 1993. *The Cure of Poetry in the Age of Prose*. Chicago: University of Chicago Press.

Kitchen, Judith. 2007. "Mending Wall." *Seneca Review* 37.2 (Spring): 47. (Reprinted in *The Fourth Genre: Contemporary Writers of/on Creative Nonfiction*, 6th ed.)

Kitchen, Judith. 2012. "The Art of Digression." In *The Rose Metal Press Field Guide to Writing Flash Nonfiction*, edited by Dinty W. Moore, 118–21. Brookline, MA: Rose Metal Press.

Knopp, Lisa. 2009. "'Perhapsing': The Use of Speculation in Creative Nonfiction." *Brevity*, January 8. https://brevitymag.com/craft-essays/perhapsing-the-use-of-speculation-in-creative-nonfiction/ (accessed December 16, 2022).

Krauth, Nigel. 2019. "Fragmented Narratives: Minding the Textual Gap." *TEXT* 23.2 (October). http://www.textjournal.com.au/oct19/krauth.htm (accessed July 27, 2022).

Lauterbach, Ann. 1999a. "On Flaws: Toward a Poetics of the Whole Fragment." In *Theory & Event* 3.1. Baltimore: Johns Hopkins University Press. Archived at https://muse.jhu.edu/article/32543.

Lauterbach, Ann. 1999b. "Q&A American Poetry: What's American About American Form?" *Poetry Society of America*. https://poetrysociety.org/poems-essays/q-a-american-poetry-1/ann-lauterbach (accessed March 7, 2022).

Lee, Li-Young. 2006. "The Pregnant Silence That Opens." In *Breaking the Alabaster Jar: Conversations with Li-Young Lee*, edited by Earl G. Ingersoll, 116–24. Rochester, NY: BOA Editions.

Lenney, Dinah. 2017. "Little Black Dress." *Chaparral (2017–18)*. http://www.chaparralpoetry.net/past-issues/object-parade-just-in-case/ (accessed April 21, 2021).

Lindner, April. 2012. "Eloquent Silences: Lyric Solutions to the Problem of the Biographical Narrative." In *The Contemporary Narrative Poem: Critical Crosscurrents*, edited by Steven P. Schneider, 102–22. Iowa City: University of Iowa Press.

Longenbach, James. 2008. *The Art of the Poetic Line*. Minneapolis: Graywolf Press.

Lopate, Phillip. 1995. *The Art of the Personal Essay*. New York: Anchor Books.

Lopate, Phillip. 2013. "The Lyric Essay" In *To Show and To Tell: The Craft of Literary Nonfiction*, 122–6. New York: Free Press.

Lowell, Amy. 1914. "Vers Libre and Metrical Prose." *Poetry: A Magazine of Verse* 3.6 (March): 213–20.

Lukeman, Noah. 2006. *A Dash of Style: The Art and Mastery of Punctuation*. New York: Norton.

Machado, Carmen Maria. 2019. *In the Dream House*. Minneapolis: Graywolf Press.

Mailhot, Terese Marie. 2018. *Heart Berries*. Berkeley: Counterpoint Press.

McHugh, Heather. 1993. *Broken English: Poetry and Partiality*. Middletown, CT: Wesleyan University Press.

McHugh, Heather. 1996. "Moving Means, Meaning Moves: Notes on Lyric Destination." In *Poets Teaching Poets: Self and the World*, edited by Gregory Orr and Ellen Bryant Voigt, 207–20. Ann Arbor: University of Michigan Press.

McSweeney, Joyelle. 2014. *The Necropastoral: Poetry, Media, Occults*. Ann Arbor: University of Michigan Press.

Miller, Brenda. 2016. "Pantoum for 1979." In *An Earlier Life*, 52–4. Port Townsend, WA: Ovenbird Books.

Miller, Brenda and Suzanne Paola, eds. 2005. *Tell It Slant: Writing and Shaping Creative Nonfiction*. New York: McGraw-Hill.

Mohabir, Rajiv. 2021. *Antiman*. Brooklyn, NY: Restless Books.

Monson, Ander. 2020. "I in River." In *I Will Take the Answer*, 24–55. Minneapolis: Graywolf Press.

Monson, Ander. 2021. "Dear Essayists Applying for an NEA." *Essay Daily*, February 16. https://www.essaydaily.org/2021/02/dear-essayists-applying-for-nea.html (accessed February 16, 2021).

Moore, Dinty W. 2013. "Positively Negative." In *Bending Genre: Essays on Creative Nonfiction*, edited by Margot Singer and Nicole Walker, 181–7. New York: Bloomsbury.

Moore, Dinty W. 2020. "On Voice, Concision, and 20 Years of Flash Nonfiction." In *Foreword to The Best of Brevity*, edited by Zöe

Bossiere and Dinty W. Moore, ix–xii. Brookline, MA: Rose Metal Press.

Ní Ghríofa, Doireann. 2020. *A Ghost in the Throat*. Windsor, ON: Biblioasis.

Noble, Randon Billings, ed. 2021. *A Harp in the Stars: An Anthology of Lyric Essays*. Lincoln, NE: University of Nebraska Press.

Nuernberger, Kathryn. 2021. *The Witch of Eye*. Louisville, KY: Sarabande Books.

O'Connor, Sheila. 2019. *Evidence of V: A Novel in Fragments, Facts, and Fictions*. Brookline, MA: Rose Metal Press.

Orr, Gregory. 1996. "Four Temperaments and the Forms of Poetry." In *Poets Teaching Poets: Self and the World*, edited by Gregory Orr and Ellen Bryant Voigt, 269–78. Ann Arbor: University of Michigan Press.

Phillips, Tom. 1980. *A Humument: A Treated Victorian Novel*. London: Thames & Hudson Ltd.

Pound, Ezra. 1913. "A Few Don'ts for an Imagiste" *Poetry: A Magazine of Verse* 1913, and "A Retrospect" *Poetry: A Magazine of Verse* 1918. Printed Together at *Poetry Foundation* website https://www.poetryfoundation.org/articles/69409/a-retrospect-and-a-few-donts (accessed July 27, 2022).

Pound, Ezra. 1914. "Vorticism." *Fortnightly Review* 96 (September): 461–71.

Preminger, Alex and T. V. F. Brogan, eds. 1993. *The New Princeton Encyclopedia of Poetry and Poetics*. Princeton, NJ: Princeton University Press.

Rankine, Claudia. 2014. *Citizen*. Minneapolis: Graywolf Press.

Rawlings, Wendy. 2014. "Let's Talk About Shredded Romaine Lettuce." *Places Journal*, March. https://placesjournal.org/article/lets-talk-about-shredded-romaine-lettuce/ (accessed August 5, 2019).

Root, Robert. 2001. "This Is What the Spaces Say." Transcript of presentation at Conference on College Composition and Communication at Kansas University, March 15. *KU Creative Nonfiction Blog*, post https://kucreativewriting.wordpress.com/recommends/readings/segmenting-this-is-what-the-spaces-say-robert-root/ (accessed March 7, 2022).

Roripaugh, Lee Ann. 2014. *Dandarians*. Minneapolis: Milkweed Editions.

Roudnitska, Edmond. 1977. *L'Esthétique en Question*. Paris: Presses Universitaires de France.

Ruefle, Mary. 2006. *A Little White Shadow*. Seattle: Wave Books.

Ruefle, Mary. 2009. Interview with Jessica Wilson. Krause Essay Prize, University of Iowa, Spring. https://krauseessayprize.org/winners-2/mary-ruefle-interview/ (accessed November 19, 2022).

Ruefle, Mary. 2012. "*My* Emily Dickinson." In *Madness, Rack, and Honey*, 143–82. Seattle: Wave Books.

Sajé, Natasha. 2012. "A Sexy New Animal: The DNA of the Prose Poem." *The Writer's Chronicle*, March/April: 33–49.
Scalzi, John. 2005. "Being Poor." *Whatever*. Weblog posting, September 3. https://whatever.scalzi.com/2005/09/03/being-poor/ (accessed December 10, 2013).
Seuss, Diane. 2021a. "[I hoisted them, two drug dealers]." In *frank: sonnets*, 67. Minneapolis: Graywolf Press.
Seuss, Diane. 2021b. "Restless Herd: Some Thoughts on Order—In Poetry, In Life." *Poets & Writers*, May/June: 39–49.
Shin, Sun Yung. 2016. *Unbearable Splendor*. Minneapolis: Coffee House Press.
Silverman, Sue William. 2009. *Fearless Confessions: A Writer's Guide to Memoir*. Athens: University of Georgia Press.
Singer, Margot and Nicole Walker, eds. 2013. *Bending Genre: Essays on Creative Nonfiction*. New York: Bloomsbury.
Tall, Deborah and John D'Agata, eds. 1997. "Foreword to *Seneca Review* (Fall 1997)." Archived online at https://www.hws.edu/senecareview/lyricessay.aspx (accessed March 7, 2022).
Tevis, Joni. 2013. "A Paperback Cabinet of Wonder: Unlocking the Long Lyric Essay." *Essay Daily*. March 25. http://www.essaydaily.org/2013/03/joni-tevis-on-long-lyric-essay.html (accessed July 27, 2022).
Thomas, Jordan K. 2015. "The Murder of Crows." *The Toast*, April 16. https://the-toast.net/2015/04/16/murder-of-crows/ (accessed December 13, 2021).
Tsai, Jennifer Lee. 2023. "The Figure of the Diseuse in Theresa Hak Kyung Cha's *Dictee* (1982): Language, Breaking Silences, and Irigarayan Mysticism." *Assay: A Journal of Nonfiction Studies* 9.2 (Spring). https://www.assayjournal.com/jennifer-lee-tsai-the-figure-of-the-diseuse-in-theresa-hak-kyung-chas-dictee-language-breaking-silences-and-irigarayan-mysticism-assay-92.html (accessed April 1, 2023).
Turin, Luca and Tania Sanchez. 2009. *Perfumes: The A—Z Guide*. New York: Penguin.
Voigt, Ellen Bryant. 1999. *The Flexible Lyric*. Athens: University of Georgia Press.
Voigt, Ellen Bryant. 2009. *The Art of Syntax: Rhythm of Thought, Rhythm of Song*. Minneapolis: Graywolf Press.
Vuong, Ocean (@ocean_vuong). 2020. "Metaphors." *Instagram Story*, November 21. https://www.instagram.com/stories/highlights/17888013988759825/?hl=en (accessed November 21, 2020).
Wagner, Vivian. 2018. "Crafting Digression: Interactivity and Gamification in Creative Nonfiction." *Assay: A Journal of Nonfiction Studies* 5.1 (Fall). https://www.assayjournal.com/vivian-wagner-crafting-digression-interactivity-and-gamification-in-creative-nonfiction-51.html (accessed March 7, 2022).

Walker, Nicole. 2013. "Fish." In *Quench Your Thirst with Salt*, 1–3. Clarksville, TN: Zone 3 Press.

Wang, Esmé Weijun. 2019. *The Collected Schizophrenias*. Minneapolis: Graywolf Press.

Was, David. 1996. Liner notes to *The X-Files: Songs in the Key of X*. Warner Bros. Records.

Washuta, Elissa. 2014. "Note." In *My Body Is a Book of Rules*, 9–14. Pasadena, CA: Red Hen Press.

Washuta, Elissa. 2021. Zoom Reading, The Raven Bookstore. Lawrence, KS, May 11.

Washuta, Elissa and Theresa Warburton, eds. 2019. *Shapes of Native Nonfiction*. Seattle: University of Washington Press .

White, Patty. 2012. "Guide to Best Orange Blossom Perfume." *Perfume Posse Blog*, October 8. https://perfumeposse.com/2012/10/08/orange-blossom-perfume-guide-2012/ (accessed January 4, 2019).

Wilkinson, Marco. 2021. *Madder: A Memoir in Weeds*. Minneapolis: Coffee House Press.

Williams, Terry Tempest. 2012. *When Women Were Birds*. New York: Picador.

Wilson, Diana. 2015. "Laces in the Corset: Structures of Poetry and Prose that Bind the Lyric Essay." *Assay: A Journal of Nonfiction Studies* 1.2 (Spring). https://www.assayjournal.com/diana-wilson-laces-in-the-corset-structures-of-poetry-and-prose-that-bind-the-lyric-essay-12.html (accessed August 13, 2019).

Wimsatt, W. K. and M. C. Beardsley. 1949. "The Affective Fallacy." *The Sewanee Review* 57.1: 31–55. JSTOR, https://www.jstor.org/stable/27537883 (accessed July 27, 2022).

SUGGESTED READING LIST

Many of these readings are covered in multiple chapters and available online:

Cha, Theresa Hak Kyung. 2001. "Diseuse." In passage of *Dictee*. Berkeley: U of CA P. https://www.degruyter.com/document/doi/10.1525/9780520945333-001/html.
Dillard, Annie. 1977. *Holy the Firm*. New York: Harper & Row. The moth passage is http://rhinehartenglish3.weebly.com/uploads/2/2/1/0/22108252/transfiguration_dillard.pdf.
Doyle, Brian. 2003. "Leap." In *Leaping: Revelations and Epiphanies*. Chicago: Loyola Press. https://www.pbs.org/wgbh/pages/frontline/shows/faith/questions/leap.html.
Doyle, Brian. 2019. "Joyas Voladoras." In *One Long River of Sound*. New York: Little, Brown and Co. https://theamericanscholar.org/joyas-volardores/.
Fish, Kathy. 2017. "Collective Nouns for Humans in the Wild." *Jellyfish Review*, October 13. https://jellyfishreview.wordpress.com/2017/10/13/collective-nouns-for-humans-in-the-wild-by-kathy-fish/.
Huber, Sonya. 2017. "What Pain Wants." In *Pain Woman Takes Your Keys*. Lincoln: U of Nebraska P. *Rogue Agent*: http://www.rogueagentjournal.com/issue11.
Mailhot, Terese Marie. 2019. "Little Mountain Woman." In *Shapes of Native Nonfiction*, edited by Therese Warburton and Elissa Washuta. Seattle: U of Washington P. *BOAAT*: http://www.boaatpress.com/little-mountain-woman.
Rankine, Claudia. 2014. *Citizen: An American Lyric*. Minneapolis: Graywolf Press. Excerpt https://www.forwardartsfoundation.org/forward-prizes-for-poetry/claudia-rankine/claudia-rankine-in-line-at-the-drugstore/.
Roripaugh, Lee Ann. 2014. "Inquiline." In *Dandarians*. Minneapolis, MN: Milkweed Editions. http://www.versedaily.org/2014/inquiline.shtml.

Seuss, Diane. 2021. "[I hoisted them, two drug dealers]." In *frank: sonnets*. Minneapolis: Graywolf Press. *Brevity*: https://brevitymag.com/nonfiction/i-hoisted-them-two-drug-dealers/

Shin, Sun Yung. 2016. "Orphan: The Plural Form." In *Unbearable Splendor*. St. Paul: Coffee House Press. https://aaww.org/orphan-plural-form/.

Walker, Nicole. 2013. "Fish." In *Quench Your Thirst with Salt*. Clarksville, TN: Zone 3 Press. *Brevity* at https://brevitymag.com/nonfiction/fish/.

INDEX

Abdurraqib, Hanif 89–90, 128, 133
 "On Marathons and Tunnels" 90
 "On Times I Have Forced Myself to Dance" 128, 133
absence 24, 29, 31–6, 42–6, 48, 88, 130. *See also* silence; white space
Ackerman, Diane, "Smell" 119
Ali, Agha Shahid 64–6
 "Ghazal: The Charms of a Considered Disunity" 64–5
 "Ghazal: To be Teased into DisUnity" 65–6
Alison, Jane 9, 21, 23–4, 26, 28, 29, 106, 110, 125–6, 135, 144–5
 Meander, Spiral, Explode: Design and Pattern in Narrative 9, 21, 23–4, 26, 29, 106, 125–6, 135, 144
alliteration 67–8, 70, 73, 81
Alvarado, Beth, "Essays All: However We Decide to Collect Them" 105–8, 111–13
Alvarez, María Isabel, "Strawberry Girl: A Prose Sestina" 98–9
amplification
 of image 92–3, 131

of meaning 14, 15, 17, 22–3, 26, 74, 92–3, 109
 of sound 74, 81, 83, 131
anaphora 17, 23, 28, 70, 71, 76, 117, 149–50
apposition 15–18, 40, 49–50, 136–7, 147
Aristotle 13, 36, 107
The Art of Syntax: Rhythm of Thought, Rhythm of Song (Voigt) 126–8, 134
The Art of the Personal Essay (Lopate) 102
The Art of the Poetic Line (Longenbach) 86, 127, 130–1
Assay: A Journal of Nonfiction Studies 1, 103–4
association. *See also* lateral moves
 associative leaps 19, 48, 86, 92–3
 associative thinking 19, 48, 86–8, 92–3, 105–6, 109–14, 117
 word associations 74, 132
assonance 70, 73

Babine, Karen 1–2, 9–13, 85, 110, 138
 "A Taxonomy of Nonfiction; Or the Pleasures of Precision" 13, 110
 "On Torque: Turns in Nonfiction" 138

INDEX

Baker, David
  Radiant Lyre: Essays on Lyric Poetry 16–17, 92, 134
  "To Think of Time" 16–17, 22
Ballenger, Bruce, "A Narrative Logic of the Personal Essay" 106
Bascom, Tim, "Picturing the Personal Essay" 106, 109
Beasley, Sandra
  "Depends on Who You Ask" 148–9
  "On Lyric Essays" 51
Beaulieu, Denyse, *The Perfume Lover* 120–1
Belcourt, Billy-Ray 129
Bending Genre: Essays on Creative Nonfiction (Singer and Walker) 38, 103
Biondolillo, Chelsea
  The Skinned Bird 112–13
  "The Story You Never Tell" 35
Biss, Eula
  interview with 19
  "Time and Distance Overcome" 15, 18, 48, 51
Bluets (Nelson) 67, 87, 116
The Body: An Essay (Boully) 34, 41, 45, 57
Bonnaffons, Amy, "Bodies of Text: On the Lyric Essay" 18, 50, 53–4, 116–17
The Book of Delights (Gay) 135
Borges, Jorge Luis 10–11
Boully, Jenny, *The Body: An Essay* 34, 41, 45, 57
braided essay
  discussion 18, 64, 97, 102, 110, 136–7, 141, 143–4, 150–1
  examples 112, 135, 138, 144, 150
Brevity 102, 131, 135, 143
Burd, Jennifer, "White Space as Metaphoric Frame" 39–40, 48–9

cadence 22, 23, 28, 30, 70, 74–6, 78–9, 82, 127–8. *See also* rhythm; stress
Cage, John
  4'33" 34, 45
  "Lecture on Nothing" 36, 45
  "Silent Sonata" 34, 45
Carson, Anne, *Nox* 48, 67
Cave, Nick 36
Cha, Sam, "*Unbearable Splendor*: Against 'Hybrid' Genre; Against Genre" 50, 57, 128
Cha, Theresa Hak Kyung, *Dictee* 29–30, 33, 47–8, 56
Chang, Victoria, *Dear Memory* 56
Christle, Heather, *The Crying Book* 116
Citizen (Rankine) 27–8, 42–3, 49, 135
coiling essay 135, 145
Coles, Katharine, "If a Body" 14, 68
collage. *See also* fragmented essay; juxtaposition; segmented essay
  discussions 37–8, 49–51, 63–4, 92–3, 135–6, 143–4
  examples 15–16, 24–5, 35, 48, 66, 95, 97
The Collected Schizophrenias (Wang) 112

"Collective Nouns for Humans in the Wild" (Fish) 18, 49–50, 131
consonance 70, 73, 76
Cortese, Claudia, "The Red Essay" 65–6
Creative Nonfiction 102
The Crying Book (Christle) 116
Czerwiec, Heidi
  "Cuir" 16, 74
  Fluid States 105, 111–12
  "Sweet/Crude" 88–9, 98

D'Agata, John 50, 54, 81, 109
  and Deborah Tall 2, 64, 87, 102, 116
  The Next American Essay 2, 116, 150
  Seneca Review 64, 87, 116, 150
Dandarians (Roripaugh) 16, 57, 98
A Dash of Style (Lukeman) 59–61
Dear Memory (Chang) 56
De Leon, Jennifer, *White Space: Essays on Race, Culture, and Writing* 43
Dennis, Carl, "The Temporal Lyric" 14, 15, 17, 22–3
density
  of image 14, 29, 67–8, 85
  of meaning 18, 22–5, 29–30, 71, 85
  of patterning 14, 29–30, 68–9, 79–80, 85, 131, 149
  of sound 14, 28–30, 68, 75, 85
Dickinson, Emily 26–7, 34, 35, 46–7, 52–3, 61–2
Dictee (Cha) 29–30, 33, 47–8, 56

Dillard, Annie, *Holy the Firm* 87–8, 102–3, 115–17
disjunction. *See also* disruption; leap; nonlinear; opposition
disjunctive essays (*see* collage; fragmented essay; nonlinear essay forms; segmented essay)
disjunctive strategies 14–15, 21–2, 28–9, 63–5, 86, 94, 136–7
disruption. *See also* disjunction
  of pattern 69, 72–3, 94, 136–7
  rupture in content 25, 65, 34, 39–40, 43–4, 50–3, 57, 136–7 (*see also* trauma)
  of time 21–2, 24, 25–6, 28–9, 86 (*see also* lyric time; nonlinear)
Donato, Susanna, "Classified" 146–7
Donne, John, *Devotions Upon Emergent Occasions* 116
Dowdy, Michael, "Elementary Primer" 146–8
Doyle, Brian 11–12, 23, 66, 83, 87, 102, 134–5, 153
  "Joyas Voladoras" 11–12
  "Leap" 23, 66, 83, 87, 102, 134–5
Dungy, Camille T., "Tell It Slant" 69–70

Eleftheriou, Joanna, "Is Genre Ever New? Theorizing the Lyric Essay in Its Historical Context" 39, 51–2, 64, 117
elegy. *See under* forms, poetic
Eliot, T.S. 39, 52, 92, 120

erasure   24, 28, 33–6, 38, 43–4, 128. *See also* white space
etymology   10, 15–16, 44, 83, 96, 120, 141
Evidence of V (O'Connor)   24–5, 32, 129–30

Fajardo, Anika, "What Didn't Happen"   18
Fish, Kathy
  "Collective Nouns for Humans in the Wild"   18, 49–50, 131
  "Fractured/Fragmented/Mosaic Flash"   41
"Fish" (Walker)   15, 66, 78–9, 88–9, 131
flash essay
  discussion   39, 41, 67, 79–80, 97–8, 102, 131, 135–6, 143–4, 150–1
  examples   32–3, 49–50, 98–9, 131, 148–50
The Flexible Lyric (Voigt)   21, 28–9, 90–2, 126–8, 144
Fluid States (Czerwiec)   105, 111–12
forms, essay. *See names of specific forms*
forms, poetic
  elegy   48, 134–6, 144
  ghazal   64–6
  haibun   97–100, 102, 111–12, 130, 154
  ode   26, 134–6, 144
  pantoum   97–103
  pastoral   53–5, 134–5
  prose poem   67, 79–80, 86, 97, 102, 127–8, 130–1, 150
  sestina   97–100
  sonnet   30, 63, 72–3, 79, 88–9, 97–100, 111–13, 134, 136, 144

"Four Temperaments and the Forms of Poetry" (Orr)   104, 107–11, 114
Fourth Genre   102
fragmentation. *See under* collage; fragmented essay; segmented essay
fragmented essay. *See also* collage; segmented essay
  discussion   10, 18–19, 22, 26, 28–9, 37–54, 63–6, 69–71, 86, 128–30, 135, 137, 143–4
  examples   15, 18, 24–5, 29, 32–3, 43–6, 48–50, 52, 55–7, 65–6, 71, 76, 128, 130, 140–1
frank: sonnets (Seuss)   26, 72, 88, 98, 113, 128, 131–3
Frost, Robert   68–9, 126–7, 152
function
  how lyric strategies function   2, 14–15, 18, 22, 37–9, 42, 47–8, 50, 70–3, 80, 85–7, 90–1, 107, 128–9
  lyric as function   22, 126–9, 136–7, 142–51
Fussell, Paul, *Poetic Meter and Poetic Form*   41–2, 69, 74

Gay, Ross, *The Book of Delights*   135
ghazal. *See under* forms, poetic
a ghost in the throat (Ní Ghríofa)   32
Glück, Louise, "Disruption, Hesitation, Silence"   44–5
Graham, Jorie, "Some Notes on Silence"   38, 47
Griffin, Susan, "Red Shoes"   150
Gross, Harvey   38–9

G'Schwind, Stephanie, "An Artful Placement of Needle Against Album" 106

haibun. *See under* forms, poetic
Harad, Alyssa, *Coming to My Senses* 120
A Harp in the Stars: An Anthology of Lyric Essays (Noble) 50, 135–6, 143–50
Heart Berries (Mailhot) 16, 71, 76–8, 80
Hemley, Robin 101
Herman, Barbara, *Scent & Subversion* 122–3
hermit crab essay
  discussion 5, 97, 102, 110, 135–6, 143–4
  examples 140, 146–7
Hirshfield, Jane, "Poetry and the Mind of Indirection" 40, 45
Hollander, John
  "Breaking Into Song: Some Notes on Refrain" 2, 70–1, 90–1
  "Garlands of Her Own" 68–9
Holy the Firm (Dillard) 87–8, 102–3, 115–17
Hopkins, Gerard Manley, "God's Grandeur" 79
Huber, Sonya, "What Pain Wants" 76, 80
hybrid
  discussion 2–3, 55–7, 61, 64, 67, 67, 90, 103, 110, 114, 142, 150–1
  examples 24–5, 29, 43–4, 47–8, 76, 98, 129–30

[I hoisted them, two drug dealers] (Seuss) 26, 72, 74–5, 88, 128, 131–3

image. *See also* patterning, visual; resonance, of image
  discussion 9–10, 14, 15, 24–6, 29, 72, 127, 155
  examples 15, 23, 26, 56, 66–70, 72, 76, 77–9, 87–90, 93, 95–6, 116, 117, 130–2, 138–9, 148–9
  "image alt-narratives" 23, 85–96, 121, 125
In Short (Kitchen and Jones) 102
In the Dream House (Machado) 32–3

journalistic essay 102, 109
"*Joyas Voladoras*" (Doyle) 11–12
Joyce, James, "Sirens" from *Ulysses* 79, 119–20
juxtaposition 1, 15–19, 22, 25–7, 48–9, 63–4, 86, 90–1, 136–9

Kincaid, Jamaica 81, 83
Kitchen, Judith 2
  "The Art of Digression" 13–14
  "Mending Wall" 2, 67–8, 81, 145, 150
  In Short 102
Knopp, Lisa "'Perhapsing': The Use of Speculation in Creative Nonfiction" 18, 31, 109–10, 146–7
Krauth, Nigel, "Fragmented narratives: Minding the textual gap" 137, 139

language. *See also* etymology; wordplay
  density of 25–6, 29–30, 75, 79–80, 85, 148–50
  diction 15, 18, 23, 31–2, 64, 80, 121–2, 131, 136–9, 146, 148, 154

failure of 43–4, 47–8, 57, 120–2, 131
music of 14, 29, 73–5, 79–80, 82, 108, 126–7
patterning of 2, 10, 15, 18, 64, 72, 74–80, 113, 125, 127, 136–7, 148–50
vs. silence 14, 26, 42, 44–5, 52–3
lateral moves 1, 9–10, 13–19, 24, 60, 111–14, 136–7
Lauterbach, Ann
 "On Flaws: Toward a Poetics of the Whole Fragment" 53
 "Q&A American Poetry: What's American About American Form?" 52, 53
leap 10–12, 19, 40, 42, 48–50, 63, 83, 86, 101–3, 138
"Leap" (Doyle) 23, 66, 83, 87, 102, 134–5
Lee, Li-Young, "The Pregnant Silence That Opens" 37, 47
Lenney, Dinah, "Little Black Dress" 18
Lindner, April, "Eloquent Silences: Lyric Solutions to the Problem of the Biographical Narrative" 64
line, poetic 15, 22, 30, 36, 38–9, 52, 62, 65, 71, 72, 74, 127–31
 and fragment 25–8, 50, 69, 71, 128–30
 vs. sentence 69, 71, 86, 98–9, 127, 130–3, 136
linear 1, 17, 21, 22, 63–4, 86, 93–4, 105, 107, 126–8, 136–7, 144

line break 15, 22, 25–6, 28, 62, 69, 128–30, 136, 154
Longenbach, James, *The Art of the Poetic Line* 86, 127, 130–1
Lopate, Philip
 The Art of the Personal Essay 102
 "The Lyric Essay" 42, 64, 103
López, Casandra, "Fragment: Strength" 149–50
Lowell, Amy, "Vers Libre and Metrical Prose" 79, 131
Lukeman, Noah, *A Dash of Style* 59–61
The Lyric Essay as Resistance (Bossiere and Trabold) 150
lyric. *See* function; lyric time; mode, lyric; nonlinear essay forms
lyric strategies 2–3, 21–9, 54, 69–70, 76, 80, 85, 90–4, 97, 128–9, 131, 134–9, 142–51. *See also specific lyric strategies*
The Lyric Theory Reader (Jackson and Prins) 117, 134
lyric time 14–15, 17, 21–30, 44, 47, 53, 60–2, 71, 82, 86, 91
 vs. narrative time 16–17, 21–5

McDowell, Robert 38–9
Machado, Carmen Maria, *In the Dream House* 32–3
McHugh, Heather 39–40
 Broken English: Poetry and Partiality 52–3
 "Moving Means, Meaning Moves: Notes on Lyric Destination" 14–15

INDEX

McPhee, John, "The Search for Marvin Gardens" 150
McSweeney, Joyelle, *The Necropastoral* 53–5
Madder: A Memoir in Weeds (Wilkinson) 25
Mailhot, Terese
  Heart Berries 16, 71, 76–8, 80
  "Little Mountain Woman" 76–8
Marano, Dawn 101
Masson, D.I., "Thematic Analysis of Sound in Poetry" 79–80
Meander, Spiral, Explode: Design and Pattern in Narrative (Alison) 9, 21, 23–4, 26, 29, 106, 125–6, 135, 144
memoir 15, 21, 66, 78, 102, 123, 144
  hybrid 24–5, 43–4, 98, 113, 129
  -in-essays 32–3, 112
metaphor 14, 28, 48, 87, 92–5, 122–3
A Midsummer Night's Dream 81, 83
Mill, John Stuart 91
Miller, Brenda 99, 101
  "Pantoum for 1979" 99
  Tell It Slant 97, 102
mode
  assay 11, 13, 21, 109–13, 144, 150
  lyric 2, 9, 11, 13–14, 21–3, 28, 68, 85–6, 90–1, 109–13, 126–8, 143–51
  narrative 13, 21–3, 90, 106, 109–11, 113, 126, 144, 146–50
Mohabir, Rajiv, *Antiman* 129

Momaday, N. Scott, *The Way to Rainy Mountain* 67
Monson, Ander
  "Dear Essayists Applying for an NEA" 103
  "I in River" 45–6, 51
Moore, Dinty W.
  Brevity 102
  Foreword to *The Best of Brevity* 102
  "Positively Negative" 18, 38, 40
motif 64, 66, 68, 72, 87–91, 94, 95, 146, 147
"*My Emily Dickinson*" (Ruefle) 26–7, 46–7

narrative. *See also* linear; story; mode, narrative
narrative essay
  discussion 1, 9–10, 101–3, 106, 109–10, 114, 137
  examples 99, 111–13, 144, 146–50
Nelson, Maggie, *Bluets* 67, 87, 116
The New Princeton Encyclopedia of Poetry and Poetics 67–8, 70–3, 79, 80
The Next American Essay 2, 116, 150
Nezhukumatathil, Aimee, *World of Wonders* 134–5, 153
Ní Ghríofa, Doireann, *a ghost in the throat* 32
Noble, Randon Billings 50, 135–7, 143–5
NonfictioNOW 101, 103
Panels
  "The Essay as Unstrung Lyre: Prosody in Nonfiction Forms" (2018) 14, 97, 103

"The Poessaytics of Form"
(2015) 97
nonlinear 9–11, 17, 21–4, 29,
63–4, 85–8, 93–4, 105–6,
117, 135–7, 143–5
nonlinear essay forms 9–11,
21–30, 86–94, 117,
135–7, 143–4
Nox (Carson) 48, 67
Nuernberger, Kathryn, *The Witch of Eye* 31

O'Brien, Timothy 81–3
O'Connor, Flannery 90
O'Connor, Sheila, *Evidence of V* 24–5, 32, 129–30
ode. *See under* forms, poetic
Olson, Charles 90
opposition 17–18, 49–50, 64, 136–7, 147
Orr, Gregory, "Four Temperaments and the Forms of Poetry" 104, 107–11, 114
Ovid 55, 88

pantoum. *See under* forms, poetic
parallelism 13, 15–17, 72–3, 91–2, 126, 132–3, 136–9, 147–50. *See also* apposition; juxtaposition
pastoral. *See under* forms, poetic
patterning
  sonic 24, 44–5, 64, 68–83, 108, 110, 113, 127, 131, 137, 149
  structural 2, 9, 11–12, 23–6, 44–6, 64–5, 68–80, 90–1, 97–9, 107–8, 110, 125–8, 131, 134–9, 143–7
  syntactical 24, 64, 69, 70, 76, 131, 137, 149

visual 44–5, 68, 113
performance 134, 136, 144, 152–5
Perfume Posse blog 122
"perhapsing" 18, 31, 109–10, 146–7
Phillips, Tom, *A Humument* 35
The Pillow Book (Shōnagon) 116
plaiting essay 135, 141, 145
Plumly, Stanley, "Lyric Time" 17, 26, 30
Poetic Meter and Poetic Form (Fussell) 41–2, 69, 74
poetics 3, 38, 53–4, 56, 64, 67–8, 91, 106–7, 109–10, 114
Pound, Ezra 45, 52
  "A Few Don'ts for an Imagiste" and "A Retrospect" 74, 92
  "Vorticism" 93
"process of mind" 16–17, 22–3, 66, 86, 90–4, 110, 125, 131
prose poem. *See under* forms, poetic
punctuation 38–9, 45, 59–62, 70, 75, 128–9, 131–2, 152
Purpura, Lia 81, 83
Pythagoras 36

Radiant Lyre: Essays on Lyric Poetry (Baker and Townsend) 16–17, 92, 134
Rankine, Claudia, *Citizen* 27–8, 42–3, 49, 135
Rawlings, Wendy, "Let's Talk About Shredded Romaine Lettuce" 56
refrain. *See also* repetition

discussion 2, 23, 26, 65, 67–71, 85, 90–1, 97–8
examples 24–6, 72, 77, 81–3, 132, 133
repetition. *See also* patterning; resonance
 discussion 12, 23–4, 26, 28–9, 64, 68–71, 73, 85–7, 90–1, 126–7, 134
 examples 24–5, 29, 66, 72, 76–8, 98–9, 132–3, 138–9, 146, 148
 resonance 30, 48, 79–80, 92, 131, 137, 143, 149, 150. *See also* repetition
 of image 2, 15, 68, 70, 76, 85–6, 110, 117, 127
 of sound 2, 67–8, 70, 74, 76, 81–3, 85–6, 110, 117, 127, 133, 152
rhyme 65, 67–9, 72–3, 77, 79, 81, 82, 88–9, 98, 127
rhythm. *See also* cadence; stress
 discussion 18, 23–4, 30, 38–9, 69–71, 74–5, 79–80, 108, 126–8, 134
 examples 18, 75, 78, 83, 128, 140
Rimbaud, Arthur 39, 88, 115
River Teeth 102, 105
Roethke, Theodore 63
Root, Robert, "This Is What the Spaces Say" 18, 34, 37–8, 49, 50, 54
Roripaugh, Lee Ann
 Dandarians 16, 57, 98
 "Dee Aster" 16
 "Inquiline" 96, 130
 Running Brush zuihitsu blog 102
Rose Metal Press
 hybrid publishing 102
 interview with editors of 142

Roudnitska, Edmond 123
Ruefle, Mary
 interview with 150
 A Little White Shadow 35, 38
 "Monument" 150
 "My Emily Dickinson" 26–7, 46–7

Sabatini Sloan, Aisha, *Dreaming of Ramadi in Detroit: Essays* 106
Sajé, Natasha, "A Sexy New Animal: The DNA of the Prose Poem" 64
Scalzi, John, "Being Poor" 17, 71, 81
Schiff, Robyn 19
segmented essay 30, 37–8, 41, 49–54, 135–9, 143–4, 146. *See also* collage; fragmented essay
Seneca Review 64, 87, 116, 150
sentence 23, 26, 29, 30, 47–8, 59, 70–2, 75, 76, 78, 80, 98–9, 125–9, 131–4, 138–9. *See also* syntax
sestina. *See under* forms, poetic
Seuss, Diane
 frank: sonnets 26, 72, 88, 98, 113, 128, 131–3
 [I hoisted them, two drug dealers] 26, 72, 74–5, 88, 128, 131–3
 "Restless Herd: Some Thoughts on Order—In Poetry, In Life" 106
Shakespeare, William 134, 144
shape 10–11, 13, 23–4, 65, 106, 111–13, 125, 134–6, 140, 144–5
Shapes of Native Nonfiction (Warburton and Washuta) 135, 145

Shin, Sun Yung
  "Exactly Like You" 43–4
  "The Hospitality of Strangers"
    15–16
  "Orphan: The Plural Form"
    44
  Unbearable Splendor 15–16,
    43, 49, 57
Shōnagon, Sei, *The Pillow Book*
    116
silence 2, 34, 37, 38, 40–2,
    44–9, 54, 87, 113, 129,
    141, 154, 155. See also
    absence; white space
Silverman, Sue William 106
The Skinned Bird (Biondolillo)
    112–13
smell 91, 119–23
sonnet. See under forms, poetic
sound effects. See amplification,
    of sound; density of,
    sound; patterning, sonic;
    resonance, of sound;
    silence; *specific names of
    sound effects*
Steele, Timothy, *All the Fun's
    In How You Say a
    Thing* 74–5
Stein, Gertrude, *Tender Buttons*
    39, 116
Stevens, Wallace 81–2
Stone, Nomi 55–6
story 9–10, 22–5, 31, 53, 90,
    107–13, 146–7, 149.
    See also mode, narrative;
    narrative essay
stress 30, 74–5, 79, 153. See also
    cadence; rhythm
structure
  vs. form 97–100, 110, 125,
    134–45
  of piece 14–17, 21–4, 51,
    53, 68–71, 85–7, 90–1,
    97–100, 107–14, 143

syntactical 29, 69, 74, 85, 90,
    125–33, 136–40
  of thinking 22, 51, 53, 70–1,
    85–6, 90–1, 99–100,
    117, 125–42, 149–50
synesthesia 122
syntax 22–4, 28–9, 59, 64,
    69–71, 75–6, 85, 90–2,
    98, 108, 125–33, 136–9,
    149–50. See also sentence;
    structure, of thinking;
    structure, syntactical

Tall, Deborah 2, 64, 87, 102,
    116
Tell It Slant (Miller and
    Paola) 97, 102
Tevis, Joni, "A Paperback
    Cabinet of Wonder:
    Unlocking the Long Lyric
    Essay" 93–4
"This Is What the Spaces Say"
    (Root) 18, 34, 37–8,
    49, 50, 54
Thomas, Jordan K., "The Murder
    of Crows" 138–9
"Time and Distance Overcome"
    (Biss) 15, 18, 48, 51
Townsend, Ann
  "A Mind for Metaphors" 28,
    92–3
  *Radiant Lyre: Essays on Lyric
    Poetry* 16–17, 92, 134
trauma 16, 24–5, 28–9, 33,
    50–1, 53–7, 66, 76–8
Tsai, Jennifer Lee 47–8
Turin, Luca 121, 122
turns 1–2, 9–13, 42, 49, 64, 69,
    78, 98, 132, 136–8
twining essay 135, 145

Unbearable Splendor (Shin)
    15–16, 43, 49, 57
University of Utah 101–3

INDEX

Vendler, Helen   134, 136–9
Voigt, Ellen Bryant
   The Art of Syntax: Rhythm of Thought, Rhythm of Song   126–8, 134
   "The Flexible Lyric"   127–8, 144
   The Flexible Lyric   21, 28–9, 90–2, 126–8, 144
   "Rethinking Adjectives"   91–2, 121
volta. *See* turns
Vuong, Ocean, "Metaphors"   93–5, 121

Wagner, Vivian, "Crafting Digression: Interactivity and Gamification in Creative Nonfiction"   40–1, 45
Walker, Nicole   101, 113–14, 153
   Bending Genre: Essays on Creative Nonfiction   38, 103
   "Fish"   15, 66, 78–9, 88–9, 131
Wang, Esmé Weijun, *The Collected Schizophrenias*   112
Washuta, Elissa
   "Note"   31–2
   Q&A with   50, 51
   Shapes of Native Nonfiction   135, 145

Wellek, René, "Genre Theory, the Lyric, and *Erlebnis*"   28
When Women Were Birds (Williams)   35, 46, 87
white space   10, 11, 14, 18, 22, 25–30, 34, 35, 37–54, 62, 70, 128–9, 136, 154
White Space: Essays on Race, Culture, and Writing (De Leon)   43
Wilkinson, Marco, *Madder: A Memoir in Weeds*   25
Williams, Terry Tempest, *When Women Were Birds*   35, 46, 87
Williams, William Carlos   39
Wilson, Diana, "Laces in the Corset: Structures of Poetry and Prose that Bind the Lyric Essay"   9, 68, 85–6, 90
Wimsatt, William K.   66, 93–4, 125
The Witch of Eye (Nuernberger)   31
Woolf, Virginia, "The Death of the Moth"   115
wordplay   16, 70, 74, 76, 79, 81, 117, 155
World of Wonders (Nezhukumatathil)   134–5, 153

www.ingramcontent.com/pod-product-compliance
Lightning Source LLC
Chambersburg PA
CBHW071425160426